MIXED

MIXED

Multiracial College Students Tell Their Life Stories

EDITED BY

**Andrew Garrod, Robert Kilkenny,
and Christina Gómez**

Cornell University Press
Ithaca and London

First published 2014 by Cornell University Press
First printing, Cornell Paperbacks, 2014

Printed in the United States of America

Library of Congress Cataloging-in-Publication Data

Mixed (Ithaca, N.Y.)
   Mixed : multiracial college students tell their life stories /
edited by Andrew Garrod, Robert Kilkenny, and Christina
Gómez.
      pages cm
   ISBN 978-0-8014-5251-2 (cloth : alk. paper)
   ISBN 978-0-8014-7914-4 (pbk. : alk. paper)
   1. Racially mixed youth—Education (Higher)—New
Hampshire—Hanover. 2. Dartmouth College—Students—
Biography. I. Garrod, Andrew, 1937– editor of compilation.
II. Kilkenny, Robert, editor of compilation. III. Gómez,
Christina, editor of compilation. IV. Title.
   LC3641.H36M59   2014
   378.1′982—dc23   2013023200

Cornell University Press strives to use environmentally
responsible suppliers and materials to the fullest extent
possible in the publishing of its books. Such materials
include vegetable-based, low-VOC inks and acid-free papers
that are recycled, totally chlorine-free, or partly
composed of nonwood fibers. For further information, visit
our website at www.cornellpress.cornell.edu.

Cloth printing   10 9 8 7 6 5 4 3 2 1
Paperback printing   10 9 8 7 6 5 4 3 2 1

In recognition of their courage, hard work, self-understanding,
and inspirational life stories, this book is dedicated to the twelve student
autobiographers whose essays are presented here.

Ray Rochester
Kemba Chase Taylor-Rodriques
Anthony Luckett
AG

Jerry, Sofia, and Lucas
CG

Contents

Preface

In a society that has long presumed stable, unitary, and bounded racial identities, how do multiracial youth forge new identities and new ideas about race? Do these adolescents encounter unique challenges as they establish their racial identities with other individuals and with institutions that presuppose a monoracial identity? How do space and place affect their identity, and how do they navigate the changing terrain? If Erik Erikson[1] and James Marcia[2] are right in their argument that late adolescence is the stage in which the individual is challenged to create an identity, is it not especially hard for individuals who are of two or more racial heritages to be at peace in their own minds and bodies, especially in a society that often forces only one racial option? *Mixed: Multiracial College Students Tell Their Life Stories* poses some of these questions and responds to them in compelling terms.

While only 51 percent of the U.S. population is currently married, and fewer people are getting married each year, marriages between spouses of different races and ethnicities are on the rise.[3] According to a 2012 Pew research study, about 15 percent of all new marriages in the United States in 2010 were interracial or interethnic, more than double the rate in 1980 (6.7 percent). The study also found that 8.4 percent of all marriages in the United States were interracial or interethnic.[4] There was also a dramatic increase in the birthrate of multiracial children from 500,000 in 1970 to more than 6.8 million in 2000.[5] By some estimates, one in five individuals may identify as multiracial by the year 2050.[6] As these trends have developed, Americans have become more open-minded about multiracial families and relationships. According to the Pew study, 43 percent of Americans say that the growing trend of biracial marriages is "a change for the better in our society," compared to 11 percent who say it has been "a change for the worse."[7] Even adolescents have been affected by the trend; in a 2012 survey, 47 percent of white teens, 60 percent of black teens, and 90 percent of Hispanic teens reported that they had dated someone of a different race.[8]

As the prevalence of multiracial families has increased, the literature has put significant emphasis on the behaviors and attitudes of mixed-race children, and research has focused on the positive aspects of being multiracial. In "Perspectives and Research on the Positive and Negative Implications of Having Multiple Racial Identities," Margaret Shih and Diana T. Sanchez contest the idea that mixed-race individuals suffer negative identity development outcomes.[9] They discuss evidence showing that the majority of multiracial individuals have positive feelings about their multiracial identity, and point out that many studies reporting high rates of depression or behavioral issues in multiracial children are primarily based on clinical populations. A 2009 *Wall Street Journal* article also discussed the benefits of being multiracial, arguing that multiracial adolescents have "the freedom to embrace both [or all] of their racial identities."[10] In a similar vein, the American Academy of Child and Adolescent Psychiatry reports that, according to recent research, "multiracial children do not differ from other children in self-esteem, comfort with themselves, or number of psychiatric problems."[11] The study of mixed-race individuals' identity formation and development is relatively new, however, and the literature remains divided on the effects of being multiracial on adolescents' self-identity and behavior.

Another body of research emphasizes the challenges that mixed-race children face. In the study mentioned earlier, Shih and Sanchez acknowledge the unique hardships that multiracial families contend with, such as "lack of social recognition, disapproval from extended family, exclusion from neighborhood and community, discrimination, and social isolation."[12] Many theories regarding multiracial identity development include a stage in which multiracial individuals feel great tension and conflict about their racial identity. Richard Udry and his colleagues, for example, report that "mixed-race adolescents show higher risk when compared with single-race adolescents on general health questions, school experience, smoking and drinking, and other risk variables."[13] Divorce statistics appear to corroborate the particular challenges that many mixed-race children face, as they hint at evidence of instability within multiracial families; a study cited in "Interracial Divorce in the U.S.: Statistics and How

Much They Matter" shows an elevated level of divorce among interracial couples compared to couples of the same race.[14]

This anthology, a qualitative exploration of the lives of twelve brave and thoughtful college students and recent graduates who reflect on the role of race in their identity formation, does not definitively answer the questions we posed earlier, nor does it take sides in the mixed-race debate. What it does do is attempt to capture the phenomenology of being mixed-race in a compelling way, and in so doing to inspire, engage, and move our readers.

The personal stories in *Mixed* are essentially memoirs in which the autobiographers—all of them current students or recent graduates of Dartmouth College—reflect on their formative relationships and influences, life-changing events, and the role their mixed-race status has played in shaping their personal identity, values, and choices. They also examine how their identities have had an impact on their choices as they enter adulthood. The contributors to this book have parents whose heritages are African American, white, Chinese, Vietnamese, Japanese, Malaysian, Iranian, Caribbean, Cape Verdean, black Puerto Rican, Bangladeshi, Native American, North African, and Danish. Although we collected these narratives on the Dartmouth campus, this book does not focus on Dartmouth per se or on the educational impact the college has had on our contributors. It focuses, rather, on these young people's evolving racial identities. Our hope is that readers of this anthology will be able to engage with the particularities and details of these stories while also connecting with the individual human experiences.

We anticipate that some readers may find that certain of these autobiographies describe a degree of tumult and dysfunction that is not a sufficiently positive or representative picture of growing up multiracial in this society. It may be that students willing to commit the amount of time and psychic energy necessary to create a publishable narrative of their lives are more likely to have a background that presses them to tell their story than their multiracial peers with a more placid history to recount. At the same time, because these students are all current or former Dartmouth College students, their stories are, by definition, tales of successfully navigating the conventional pathways to success in American society, and in that sense a positive depiction of multiracial development. Indeed, some of their stories are at once heartrending and heartwarming, and while they do not in all cases paint a positive picture of the multiracial experience, on balance they reveal true lives behind the research data and often dry academic debates.

Almost all of the essays in this book were written since 2009. Only two, "Finding Zion" and "A Little Plot of No-Man's-Land," are older. Eight of the twelve authors worked one-on-one with Andrew Garrod in weekly one-hour meetings over the course of a ten-week term; work with the other four contributors was conducted via email. Typically, a writer would submit seven or eight pages to Garrod prior to each meeting, and these pages would be the focus when they met. Teacher and writer also discussed how to proceed with the next portion of the narrative. Garrod did not assume that a story was already formulated in a contributor's mind, and he conveyed to the writer that each story had to be uncovered piece by piece. Because the emphasis was on process—that is, on the complex task of helping writers find their voice—no editorial interventions were made during the generative stage. Although we, the editors, necessarily had established parameters, we encouraged the writers to develop their own themes and to make sense of their experiences in ways that had significant meaning for their own lives. Not infrequently, a writer was halfway through the process before he or she came to understand what the essay's central concerns and themes were. As William Zinsser observes: "Memoir writers must manufacture a text, imposing narrative order on a jumble of half-remembered events. With that feat of manipulation, they arrive at a truth that is theirs alone, not quite like that of anybody else who is present at the same events."[15]

In helping our authors articulate their stories, we offered a few guiding questions:

- What gets you up in the morning? What is most important in your life? What do you live for? What is of transcendent value to you?
- Have there been critical incidents in your life (e.g., religious conversion, parents' divorce, death in the family, first love) after which nothing was quite the same—for good or ill, or for some mixture of the two?
- Explore the most important relationships in your life—within the family and outside it.
- What sort of child were you? Did you have a particular role within your family?
- What were you like in your early years at school? Were you popular? If so, with whom? Were you a lonely child? Did any teacher pick you out as promising?
- Were you an early or late developer as you moved into adolescence? Or did you move at about the normal pace? If you were an early developer, how do you think it affected the way people saw you?

- In high school, did you develop any particular skill or interest that made you stand out? Were your best friends of the same race and ethnicity as you?
- Discuss one or two of the most significant friendships you had in your later high school years.
- When you were a child, was race/ethnicity discussed at home? If so, in what way? When were you aware that you had a "minority heritage"? Have you been the victim of racism? If so, describe the first incident: How did you feel? How did you react? How did you come to terms, if you did, with this racism?
- Why did you come to Dartmouth? What were you looking for? Was this environment much more or much less diverse than your home or high school environment?
- Has this been a supportive community for you? Have you been active in organizations that are concerned with issues of race and ethnicity? If so, how and why? If not, why not?
- As you think of moving on from Dartmouth, how do you see yourself moving into the outside world? Do you think your sense of racial identity has been strengthened in the last few years? What is the role of ethnic/racial identity within your total identity? (For some students, other aspects of identity may be more significant than race.)
- Does being multi-/biracial help you understand racial dynamics in this culture in a more profound way than monoracial individuals can?
- Please describe both the advantages and disadvantages of being multi-/biracial.
- Do you identify with one component of your racial background more than the other? If so, which one, why, and what are the perspectives or insights on life that identity provides?
- Do you sometimes switch styles/dialects/attitudes according to which racial group you are relating to? If so, please describe when, why, and how you feel about making such adjustments.
- How do people of the non-Caucasian aspect of your racial background relate to you racially? For example, if you are racially black and white, how do black people relate to you in terms of racial affinity? What effect does your racial background have on these relationships?
- In contrast with the preceding question, what aspect of your racial heritage do white people relate to? For example, does the "one-drop" rule apply, in which Caucasians perceive you racially only in terms of your minority racial background?

Further probes were available, and the exact wording was changed to reflect the heritage of the writer's parents:

- How do you self-identify?
- Have you ever seen yourself as white?
- What is your relationship to your white mother?
- What effect does it have on you that your mother is white?
- Does the quality of the relationship with your white mother in any way affect your willingness to recognize or incorporate her white heritage?
- How does the family play out race in the household?
- Do any of your siblings self-identify differently from the way you do?
- Have you ever felt people were attracted to you because of your race?
- When do you feel your minority status? When do you feel black, Asian, etc.? Are you a different person in different social settings?
- In situations when there is overt racism, do you speak out? What do you do?
- How do other people see you racially? How do you see yourself? How is it different from the way your family/siblings see you and themselves?
- Do you "pass" for being monoracial? Are you able to "pass"? Do you try to "pass"? Do people "pass" you automatically? Are you sometimes aware of other people's projections onto you?
- How do you think about race and potential partners?

These questions were offered as prompts or probes. Many of our writers chose to engage some of the questions, and others found their own inspiration.

The completed manuscripts were usually thirty-five to fifty pages. After careful consultation and discussion over months or, for some writers, even years, cutting and editing reduced and sharpened the texts to a more manageable fifteen to twenty-four pages. Our changes to the text were in most cases minimal. Variations in tone, degree of self-analysis, and style of expression reflect our commitment to respect each author's story and life.

After a draft was reduced from its original length to approximately twenty-five pages, it was sent to Robert Kilkenny, who had not worked directly with the students and therefore could offer a more objective reaction to their essays. This was done to bring the essays to another level of psychological cohesion, in the hope that areas that seemed to be avoided or mysteriously unaddressed could be brought to the writer's attention.

Kilkenny suggested how and why a story would be better understood if some of these lacunae were explored more thoroughly. He also did this to push the writers to the edge of their ability to reflect on their own life histories. It was not unusual for a writer to balk, or to say that further exploration was too painful, or that he or she was genuinely unable to reflect further about experiences that were still raw and unresolved.

Most of the students represented in this book were enrolled in one or another of Andrew Garrod's education classes, which are largely informed by a psychological developmental perspective. A few of the writers were recommended to the editors by other students and faculty. The twelve essays, six by men and six by women, represent fewer than half of those that were started. Some students withdrew their essays because they did not have the permission of their family members or friends to write about them in such personal terms; for others, the writing of the essay and the self-reflection it had prompted were the primary reason they had embarked on the adventure, and they had little interest in being published. Others hesitated to make the suggested changes or to engage in further self-exploration and editing. In such cases we made an editorial decision as to whether a piece could stand on its own without further effort or whether it was insufficiently coherent to merit publication. For a few of the writers, life intervened and they found that they did not have the time or inclination to continue making what was an enormously demanding investment of energy and time. For all of the essays so diligently worked on over the years, whether they are included in the book or not, the editors are deeply grateful.

To encourage the frankest possible examination of their lives, relationships, and the role of faith in shaping their attitudes and behavior, we insisted that the writers be given the option to maintain their anonymity if they wished to do so. Some of the contributors would not have committed themselves to paper and to such a personal exploration had we not guaranteed anonymity for them and/or the other people mentioned in their essays. Accordingly, details of identity and location have been altered in some of the memoirs. In all cases, the writer was asked to sign off on his or her section of the book manuscript.

For many of the authors, the process of putting their experiences into words has acted as a catalyst for further self-reflection on their life history. In twenty years of encouraging this type of work, the editors have consistently observed that the process of autobiographical writing can have a profoundly transformative effect on the spiritual, moral, and emotional domains of a writer's life, and that a life is often changed by such deep introspection. We have found would-be contributors overwhelmingly open to the invitation to make sense of their childhood and adolescent experiences, which up to then had been inchoate and unintegrated. This opportunity to reflect can often reconcile students to trauma they have experienced and bring emotional resolution and understanding to the primary relationships and vicissitudes in their lives. We feel deeply privileged to be guiding student writers through deeper levels of self-understanding and helping them gain purchase on their world through self-analysis and articulation.

We, the editors, are profoundly grateful to many student researchers and assistants, friends, and associates for the realization of this book. Nora Yasumura, the adviser to Asian and Asian American students, was an unflagging supporter of our project and suggested potential student contributors. Dody Riggs, so critical to many of our other student anthology projects, offered essential editorial suggestions as the manuscripts achieved their final form. Also essential to the completion of this manuscript have been the organizational, administrative, and computer skills of a number of Dartmouth students, some of whom are now alumni: Dennis Zeveloff, Trevor King, Alex Caron, Lamar Moss, Tien-Tien Jong, Justice Amoh, Richard Waitumbi, Victor Lekweuwa, William Kuzma, Taylor Malmsheimer, Richard Addo, Andrew Nalani, and Karolina Krelinova. All have helped to markedly improve the text, organize the editors, and prepare the manuscript for publication—none more so than Tien-Tien Jong.

Even under the cover of anonymity, it is not easy to open your life and your reflections on that life to public inspection. We wish to recognize all those students who have written, under their own names or under pseudonyms, with such courage and commitment in bringing their personal stories of identity into the public domain.

Notes

1. Erik Erikson, *Childhood and Society* (New York: Norton, 1993).
2. James Marcia, "Ego Identity Development," in *The Handbook of Adolescent Psychology*, ed. Joseph Adelson (New York: Wiley, 1987).
3. Wendy Wang, "The Rise of Intermarriage: Rates, Characteristics Vary by Race and Gender," Pew Research Center, Washington, D.C., 2012.
4. Ibid.
5. Margaret Shih and Diana T. Sanchez, "Perspectives and Research on the Positive and Negative Implications of Having Multiple Racial Identities," *Psychological Bulletin* 131.4 (2005): 569.
6. Jennifer Lee and Frank D. Bean, "America's Changing Color Lines: Immigration, Race/ Ethnicity, and Multiracial Identification," *Annual Review of Sociology* 30 (2004): 221–42.

7. See Wang, "Rise of Intermarriage."
8. Ibid.
9. See Shih and Sanchez, "Perspectives and Research," 569–91.
10. Sue Shellenbarger, "New Study Sheds Light on Experiences of Mixed-Race Kids," *Wall Street Journal*, June 4, 2009.
11. "Multiracial Children," Facts for Families, American Academy of Child and Adolescent Psychiatry, March 2011, http://www.aacap.org/cs/root/facts_for_families/multiracial_children.
12. See Shih and Sanchez, "Perspectives and Research," 569.
13. Richard J. Udry, Rose M. Li, and Janet Hendrickson-Smith, "Health and Behavior Risks of Adolescents with Mixed-Race Identity," *American Journal of Public Health* 93.11 (2003): 1865.
14. "Interracial Divorce in the U.S.: Statistics and How Much They Matter," *GoriGirl.com*, December 3, 2009.
15. William Zinsser, *Inventing the Truth: The Art and Craft of Memoir* (New York: Mariner, 1998), 6.

MIXED

Introduction

Esperanza Spalding, a young jazz musician, won the 2011 Grammy for Best New Artist, eclipsing the wildly popular teenage idol Justin Bieber. Information about Spalding exploded on the Internet. Who was this little-known artist? Where did she come from? Discussion of her music and her mixed-race heritage quickly filled the blogs. During an interview Spalding described her family background as reflecting "the racial balance of the future." Her father is African American; her mother is Welsh, Native American, Hispanic, and African American. Like Esperanza Spalding, a growing number of Americans describe themselves as being mixed-race, multiracial, of mixed heritage, or as having many backgrounds—black and white, Jamaican and English, Mexican and Danish, and numerous other combinations. This includes well-known figures such as Lani Guinier, Alicia Keyes, Malcolm Gladwell, Jessica Alba, and even President Barack Obama.

Most of us have a mixed ancestry. In fact, when investigating their ancestry, many people find that their forebears included people of different races—which is sometimes unexpected and often surprising to discover. In the United States, it is estimated that at least one-quarter of African Americans have an ancestor who is not of African descent.[1] The renowned Harvard professor Henry Louis Gates Jr., who appeared in the PBS series *African American Lives*,[2] found that his ancestry was more than 50 percent European—Irish, to be specific. Yet it is only since the 1980s that individuals have been able to declare their mixed-race identity publicly. Up to that time, most individuals of color were classified according to their "minority" status. Because of this hypodescent,[3] multiracial individuals defaulted to their nonwhite parentage and identified only as black,

Latino, Native American, or Asian. Today this has changed, and the option of identifying with more than one racial heritage has become a viable choice for three specific reasons. First, the U.S. Supreme Court decision in *Loving v. Commonwealth of Virginia*[4] declared the Virginia statute barring interracial marriage to be unconstitutional. Second, the efforts of a multiracial movement during the 1980s and 1990s pressed for the inclusion of a multiracial category on the 2000 U.S. Census.[5] And third, there has been a growing national acceptance for seeing ourselves in terms of greater racial complexity.

Nevertheless, choosing which term to use for individuals who identify as being of more than one race proves difficult. The descriptive language employed over time to designate race has been inconsistent. Historically, words such as *mulatto, mixed-blood,* and *half-breed* have been used to describe people of mixed race, but these terms are now generally considered outdated and unacceptable.[6] Today, *biracial, children of interracial marriages, interethnic, mixed-race,* and *multiracial* are among the terms used in indexes, catalogs, books, magazines, and newspaper articles to define this population. Some individuals have created new terms to describe themselves, like *Cablinasian,* the term Tiger Woods uses to describe his mixed heritage, which includes Caucasian, black, American Indian, and Asian.

Much has been written about which term should be used to describe people of more than one race.[7] Borrowing from Maria Root's pioneering work on mixed-race populations, we use the term *multiracial* to describe "people who are of two or more racial heritages." Root adds, "It is the most inclusive term to refer to people across all racial mixes.".[8] Our book explores the experiences of individuals who identify themselves as multiracial, and considers what this identity means for their everyday existence.

The concept of multiracial identity also raises concerns about the reification of race itself. Being multiracial assumes that there is such a thing as a single, monoracial, or "pure" racial category. Although race was once considered biological and innate, today it is understood as a social construction that has changed over time; in other words, race is not biological. Nevertheless, racial categories have evolved over the decades, and they do hold social meaning. In the social sciences, race is understood as a variable that has strong economic, political, and educational significance that can affect an individual's life chances. So even though we understand that race is "a product of human invention like fairies, leprechauns, banshees, ghosts and werewolves," it does matter as a "cultural creation" and has consequences for how a person experiences life every day.[9] Furthermore, race categories in the United States are hierarchical, and whiteness is privileged. As the activist and antiracist Tim Wise points out: "We live not only in a racialized society, but also a class system, a patriarchal system, and one in which other forms of advantage and disadvantage exist. These other forms of privilege mediate, but never fully eradicate, something like white privilege.... [T]he fact remains that when all other factors are equal, whiteness matters and carries with it great advantage."[10] Consequently, for multiracial individuals, the "mix" matters. *How* one looks (skin color, hair texture, body type, etc.) will position an individual along the continuum of racial privilege. Multiracial individuals with more European-looking features will have more privilege than African- or indigenous-looking multiracials. In the United States, race still structures access to opportunities: nonwhite children suffer substantially higher rates of poverty, attend schools with far fewer resources, and lack preventive health care.[11] Thus, having a mixed racial background can provide insight into how race in its many dimensions is understood.

The growth of the multiracial population has also spurred neoconservative activists to reiterate the idea that the United States has become a color-blind nation and that race no longer influences life chances; the mere fact that "multiracialness" exists is proof that racism and discrimination no longer pervade our society, and fuels a race-neutral doctrine.[12] Yet Jennifer Lee and Frank D. Bean's findings suggest that black multiculturalism, in particular, "continues to constitute a fundamental racial construction in American society. Hence, it is not simply that race matters, but more specifically, that black race matters, consistent with the African American exceptionalism thesis."[13] Thus, even in the case of multiracials, race still matters.

Who Is Multiracial? The U.S. Census

According to Kim Williams, the multiracial movement of the 1980s and 1990s prompted a restructuring of American racial classifications. Beginning with the 2000 U.S. Census, respondents who previously were permitted to mark only one racial category were allowed for the first time to check multiple categories; a "multiracial" category was never added, however.[14]

The ability to "mark one or more"—people were allowed to mark up to fifteen boxes—radically changed the way race was perceived in the United States. People's responses could now reflect their diverse racial backgrounds and perceptions of race itself. Although this change was groundbreaking and provoked a great deal of debate about how individuals should fill out the form, only 2.4 percent, or 6.8 million respondents, identified themselves on the 2000 census as having more than one race.

Of the census respondents who selected more than one racial category, 93.29 percent checked only two boxes; fewer than half a million respondents checked more than three. This low percentage surprised many researchers and journalists who believed that the concept of race, as a single, innate, and unchanging category, had changed. According to Joel Perlmann and Mary C. Waters, "by allowing individuals to report identification with more than one race, the census challenges long-held fictions and strongly defended beliefs about the very nature and definition of race in our society."[15]

During the 2000 enumeration, there was a strong campaign to have people check only one box even if they understood that they had a mixed racial heritage. Questions about how multiracials were going to be counted, either in aggregate or in racial combinations, had not yet been determined, though the answers matter for civil rights and voting rights, as well as social and educational programs.[16] Although the census and other surveys that classify individuals racially now seek to identify those who are multiracial as such, many mixed-race individuals do not mark more than one box. For example, on the 2010 U.S. Census, the popular press reported, President Obama marked only one box: "Black, African Am., or Negro." Many factors can influence how multiracial individuals choose to identify, including family structure, socialization, cultural or personal knowledge about one's heritage, gender, social networks, and physical appearance.[17] Some individuals who understand themselves privately as mixed-race also recognize that their race matters publicly, politically, organizationally, and in terms of the distribution of social resources. According to G. Reginald Daniel and Josef Manuel Castañeda-Liles:

> The most significant opposition [to checking more than one box] came from various African American leaders and organizations. Acknowledging that most, if not all, African Americans have some European and, in many cases, Native American ancestry, they feared many individuals would designate themselves as "multiracial" in order to escape the continuing negative social stigma associated with blackness. This, in turn, would reduce the number of individuals who would be counted as black, which would affect the ability to track historical and contemporary patterns of discrimination and enforce civil rights initiatives. Similar concerns were expressed from other communities of color.[18]

The 2010 U.S. Census saw the number of people who marked two or more races rise to approximately 9 million, or 2.9 percent of the population. This was a 32 percent increase from 2000. Every state except New York showed an increase in its multiracial population since 2000, and some states saw a significant rise, such as North Carolina (100%), South Carolina (100%), Delaware (83%), Georgia (81.7%), and West Virginia (71.9%). Yet the percentage of people who marked more than one box was still small; 97 percent of all respondents (299.7 million) still marked only one race. In other words, approximately one in forty U.S. residents identified as multiracial in 2010. Some estimate, however, that by 2050 the ratio could be one in five, or about 20 percent of the U.S. population.[19] Whatever is to come by the middle of the twenty-first century, the data from the 2000 and 2010 censuses show that racial identity is fluid, contextual, and both a private and a public phenomenon.

Stories of Being Multiracial

The students who contributed to this volume negotiate their race in various situations; they often present one identity one day and another the next. The notion of checking one or more boxes fails to capture the realities experienced by mixed-race individuals. Surveys provide a demographic portrait, but they do not portray life experiences. These essays, written in the voices of multiracial students, explore the concerns these young people confront with their families and friends in their everyday lives, and as they enter adulthood.

Each chapter in this book reveals a story of how race is lived within the context of being multiracial. Unlike individuals who understand themselves as having one racial identity, these students have lived the complexity of their identity from a very young age. They understand how their mixed racial identity impacts their lives, how the race of their parents and other family members affects their childhood development, and how others' understanding of them shapes their relationships. For these young adults, negotiating their identity is an everyday occurrence, one that often causes stress, and at times one that offers them the privilege of seeing their environment from a different perspective.

The essays in this collection are organized according to three main themes. The first section—"Who Am I?"—focuses on the question of identity and self-exploration. Students write about their struggle to fit in at various points in their lives and to discover where they belong.

They are reminded that they are different by the questions strangers ask about their race, or when trying to decide how to self-identify. The second section—"In-Betweenness"—explores the students' concerns about feeling caught in the middle between their parents' two worlds, about being part of each but belonging fully to neither. The third section—"A Different Perspective"—highlights how their multiracialism gives these students a unique lens through which to view their environment. This different perspective often helps them navigate their world. Their multiracial identity underscores the multiple identities these students inhabit: they are also gay, immigrants, undocumented, poor, or wealthy; their multiracial identity is but one of many they must manage as they pass through late adolescence.

Who Am I?

The authors of the stories in this section—Ana Sofia De Brito, Chris Collado, Yuki Kondo-Shah, and Allison Bates—share their insights regarding their difference through the questions others ask about their identity. Because their physical appearance does not place them clearly in a known racial category, these students are regularly asked, "What are you?" Moreover, how they understand themselves is not always how others view them. This dissonance between their self-identification and others' understanding of who they are grows tiresome for them.

In her essay, "Good Hair," Ana Sofia Brito struggles with her racial identification. Questions of racial identity are tied to the history and location of her Cape Verdean family. Her tan skin, curly (but not kinky) hair, and thin nose cause her to be viewed as black, white, or even Latina in the United States. Among Cape Verdeans, Ana Sofia doesn't have to explain who she is, but in the United States, her identity causes confusion: "In America, I often feel I'm forced to choose whether I'm black or white or "other." I prefer to choose "other" because I'm neither black nor white, but being in between creates problems for others trying to classify me. So here in the United States I identify as black, which is the most comfortable category to fit myself into, but I constantly feel like the immigrant stepchild to black American culture." But Ana Sofia's racial identification as black puzzles her family, who insist that she is white, since the history of her family and their native country privileges whiteness. Concepts of *melhorar a raça*, bettering the race by marrying a white or lighter-skinned individual, is a long-established practice in many parts of the world, in particular those that are former Portuguese and Spanish colonies. Ana Sofia's family does not understand why she would not identify as white, given that she doesn't necessarily look black, especially by Cape Verdean standards.

Still, in the United States—where, according to the "one-drop rule," having any African ancestry makes one black—Ana Sofia can be identified as black and chooses to do so. Interestingly, in order to be accepted as black, she adopts accents and mannerisms in order to appear "more black." For Ana Sofia, like many multiracial individuals, the understanding that race is a social construct is a lived experience. Students learn early on that if you are going to adopt a racial identity that is not so apparent to others, then you must also adopt racial artifacts to "perform" that racial identity. Thus, by wearing her hair curly rather than straightened, allowing herself to get tanned to appear darker-skinned, and taking classes in the African American studies department, Ana Sofia appears "more black," more authentic. Yet she still often feels lost: "After three years at college, I still feel there is a divide between dark-skinned and light-skinned blacks, and between African Americans and Africans. Interestingly, I am African and I identify mostly with African American culture, yet I feel as if I'm not being taken seriously at black group events because of my light skin." Consequently, the question "Who am I?" is not settled for Ana Sofia, and she hopes for a future when she will not have to choose.

In "So, What Are You?" Chris Collado, whose father is Afro-Cuban and whose mother is white, relates his reaction to the types of questions he often receives about his ancestry:

"Are you black?" "I thought you were Mexican because you speak Spanish, right?" "So, what are you?" These are the types of questions I have answered my entire life. I used to get annoyed when people would ask me "What are you?" in a tone similar to one you might use to ask about a homemade Halloween costume. I have been mistaken for being black, Mexican, Italian, and, on one occasion, Greek. I even had an older woman once ask me, "Has anyone ever told you that you look like Pete Sampras?"... It can be so frustrating to have the very part of you that makes you unique ignored. For the longest time I couldn't understand why people saw me as anything but biracial or, the more socially recognized term, "mixed."

His physical features—light brown complexion, brown eyes, and thick curly hair—make Chris a curiosity. His ability to speak Spanish throws an additional curveball at those who try to categorize him; he doesn't fit clearly into a stereotypical black or Latino box. Chris understands himself as mixed-race and wonders why others cannot see him the same way.

This kind of identity dissonance is amplified in these students' relationships with their parents. Because children of mixed racial heritage do not always look like their parents, the two generations can have quite different experiences. As children enter adolescence, they begin to understand that their racial identity might be viewed differently in their environment than it is in their parents', and that their experiences are often dissimilar. In her 1996 article "Brown-Skinned White Girls," France Winddance Twine examines the relationships between multiracial female college students who have African ancestry and their nonblack mothers. As these young women entered university, some found that their mothers were not always able to participate in a knowledgeable way in discussions about racial identity and racism.[20]

For Yuki Kondo-Shah, who is Japanese and Bangladeshi, understanding who she is includes not only racial differences but also cultural differences. She was raised in Japan until age seven, when her family moved to the United States. Though an American citizen, she understands herself as being Japanese, but she doesn't "look" Japanese. During her summer visits to Japan, Yuki learns quickly that her assimilation back into Japanese culture will not be so simple: "As time went on, I found that I didn't fit into Japanese society anymore because I was 'too American,' but I didn't fit into American culture either because I was 'too foreign.' I had become someone without a home, and that was terribly isolating. The Japanese label I longed to stick on my forehead didn't match those being placed on me without my consent." Being neither Japanese nor American gives her a sense of not belonging, of being an outsider to both groups. Not feeling authentic enough, Yuki chooses not to join Asian student organizations while at college. She worries about being seen as "a fake or a poser." This feeling of being thought inauthentic and facing suspicion and even antagonism has been well documented.[21] After college, Yuki faces her fears by studying the history of various Asian ethnic groups in order to feel comfortable with her place in the world. Now in graduate school, she understands herself in a more "sophisticated" way, knowing that who she is includes her many experiences and cultures.

In her essay, "A Sort of Hybrid," Allison Bates questions whether her white mother struggles with the same issues that she does:

> I often wonder if my mom ever grappled with how to check the "race box"
> when it came to the forms and documents she surely had to fill out for all of
> her kids. Which one did she choose: white, black, or other? Or did she write

in something else? I don't really know the answer to these questions because I've never asked, which reveals a large gap in my understanding of how my mother sees herself in her own family. I have often felt foreign and out of place when I am with her side of the family, which leads me to wonder if my mother feels uncomfortable about being the only white person in our immediate and extended family. Even though I am technically half white, I don't feel it; I don't even know if I'm supposed to. I have no concept of what it must be like never really to have to be aware of your difference. I think that is because, as a society, we see whiteness as racelessness.

Allison, like other students in this book, understands that her parents occupy a different racial space than she does, which causes a disconnection between them. "Who am I?" becomes a difficult question to answer, because children often use their parents as reference points; children view themselves as a reflection of their parents and vice versa, but when children and parents identify with different racial categories, the question "Who am I?" becomes more complicated. Consequently, the racial socialization of multiracial children becomes challenging for parents, as Kerry Ann Rockquemore, Tracey Laszloffy, and Julia Noveske explain:

> In same-raced families, the focus of racial identity development is to try to encourage children to have a positive perspective on their blackness in spite of the pervasive societal devaluation of blackness. In short, there is an assumption that the child is black, and parents work to build a positive black identity. However, in black/white interracial families, the child can identify as black, white, biracial, or as no race. This sets up a situation in which parents need to be in alignment with consistent messages about his or her racial group membership.[22]

This "alignment" is not always easy to achieve, especially when children are often asked "What are you?" or when parents are asked "Did you adopt your child?" For the authors of these stories, the inconsistent messages about their identity do cause frustration, and at times even detachment from their families. Moreover, because these students have not quite reached adulthood, their understanding of themselves is still developing.

In-Betweenness

All the students in this book learned early on that they are part of two or more cultures. Whether it is because of the way they look or because of their different family heritages, they understand that they inhabit a separate space that is often "in between." The students in this section—Shannon Joyce Prince, Thomas Lane, Ki Mae Ponniah Heussner, and Samiir Bolsten—articulate their sense of being in the middle.

In *Raising Biracial Children*, Rockquemore and Laszloffy examine how mixed-race people understand their racial identity and challenge the assumption that there is only one appropriate way to identify one's race. They argue that one of the greatest challenges mixed-race people confront arises when the identity they choose is rejected by others in their community.[23] The students who tell their stories in this book understand firsthand this struggle with being in between and part of many heritages. Like a Venn diagram, they are the intersections of the various circles, an element that is made from many sets. Shannon Joyce Prince, in her essay "Seeking to Be Whole," describes her multiple identities:

> Whenever I've been called on to define my heritage, I've never been perplexed about how to answer. My response has not changed since I was first able to speak, just as my ethnic identity has never shifted. When asked what I am, I smile and say, "I am African American, Cherokee (Aniyunwiya) Native American, Chinese (Cantonese) American, and English American." I excise nothing of myself. I claim the slave who was a mathematical genius; the storyteller, the quilt maker, and the wise healer; the bilingual railroad laborer and the farmer—regardless of the amount of melanin in any of their skins.

Her words are strong and clear and reflect the identity that she chose for herself early in life, which she defends firmly. Like Rockquemore and Laszloffy, Prince understands identity as a social process. She does not try to "fit" into a single correct identity but proudly shares her understanding that she is between and part of all her many heritages.

That liminal space, however, is adaptable and contextual, as Thomas Lane describes in his essay, "The Development of a *Happa*." He writes: "I am a *happa*, a Hawaiian word for someone who is half Asian. I can be white, I can be Asian, or I can be somewhere in between, depending on what suits me at the time. ...I am and always have been living in two separate worlds. I was the white boy eating fermented soybeans, the Asian boy who could speak English, and the jock who played card games." He understands that he can be chameleon-like and change with the situation. Although he might sometimes be forced to "pick one side," he can transform himself later. His ability to move between two cultures makes him feel as though he does not fit in, but with time he hopes to close the gap between his Japanese and American sides and "feel equally comfortable with both cultures and be able to switch between them naturally."

Ki Mae Ponniah Heussner, in "A Little Plot of No-Man's-Land," also wrestles with belonging to the two different cultures of her parents. She writes:

> When I feel inextricably caught between their two worlds—rejected by both, or too quickly accepted by one—I wish to be solely of one heritage. I do not think people often realize how much of a luxury it can be to have one group to fall back on, one to blame, or one to identify with and one to reject. Perhaps it's easier to wear your racial consciousness on your sleeve when you know that you can always hide behind the garb of an entire race if things get too bad, or if the opposition comes on a little bit too strong for you alone. Most will never know how much more difficult it is to speak out when you feel as though you have to pick a side, even though *neither* side is really your own.

Belonging to neither and not having one reference group to call upon adds stress to Ki Mae's everyday interactions. In their seminal book *Beyond Black: Biracial Identity in America*, Kerry Ann Rockquemore and David L. Brunsma use the category "border identity" to describe biracial individuals who consider themselves to be not a part of either parent's racial categories but a "unique hybrid category of self-reference."[24] Moreover, these individuals have two kinds of border identities: those that are validated by others and those that are not. Ki Mae describes having just such a border identity; at times she is validated and at other times she is not. Like other students in our book, Ki Mae feels she is in between.

Sometimes this "in-betweenness" leads our authors to feel different from other people. In his essay, "Finding Blackness," Samiir Bolsten relates how he has handled difficult circumstances:

> I was used to dealing with awkward and offensive situations related to race, having grown up with my dark complexion in predominantly white Denmark. Later on, as my family moved to more diverse environments, perceptions of me changed—both in my own eyes and in the eyes of others. It seemed that because of my unusual family situation and racial makeup, I was always perceived as different from the norm, no matter where we relocated. Although this led to issues of low self-worth and some turbulent times mentally, I eventually became comfortable with always being different. Much of

this comfort came from realizing that norms were by no means rules, and that all people had some way in which they were different.

Samiir's comfort with "being different" makes him wiser and better able to comprehend how he is being judged. Being multiracial offers all these students a different perspective from which to understand their experiences.

A Different Perspective

In their essays in this section, the students discuss how being multiracial affords them a different perspective on a given situation from that of their friends or family members who are monoracial. Being different or in between in fact makes them aware of their unique vantage point. Because questions about their race or background come up often, they have thought about these issues in ways that their friends perhaps have not. They strive to become their own individuals. They are young people who are developing an understanding of who they are, including their sexual orientation, political affiliation, and future profession. In "Chow Mein Kampf," Taica Hsu, who is Asian, white, and gay, explains his concern about his many identities:

> I still struggle with the perception of my race in the gay male community and my own attraction to full-Asian gay men. . . . As a result, I have become hypersensitive to the reasons why gay men are or are not attracted to me: Do they like me because I am exotic (half Asian)? Do they not like me because I look too Asian? How do I cover my more effeminate (read: Asian) characteristics and features? . . . I hope to overcome these hurdles in time and fully accept my mixed racial background. Then, and only then, will my gay identity and racial identity truly exist in harmony.

Hsu is trying to synthesize his many sides, but his multiracialism might make that task more complicated. The intersection of his multiracial identity and his sexual orientation affects how he sees himself and possibly how others view him as well.

Anise Vance, in "A Work in Progress," describes how his Iranian–African American ancestry allows him to move in different spaces—Kenya, Egypt, and the United States. Although the transitions are not always easy, Anise's unique position as multiracial and multicultural gives him insights into his own identity and that of others. Anise writes: "I was eager to explore the identity choices I found laid before me. Scholars and analysts often talk of 'negotiating' or 'navigating' identity. Clothing, speech patterns, hairstyles, rebelliousness, athleticism, flirtatiousness—all are used to project identity. Everyone navigates identity, but when race is introduced into the mix, the stakes are raised. At an early age I learned how to twist my self-presentation to provoke specific responses from those around me." Anise's cultural code-switching—that is, his ability to navigate in different surroundings—enables him to represent himself in a way that he controls and can benefit from.

Dean O'Brien, in "We Aren't That Different," eloquently describes the benefits of being multiracial: "I know that my mixed racial heritage has colored my experiences in many ways, but I think it does so in a way that isn't exclusive to race. Because I have grown up with two different cultures, the idea that there are multiple valid perspectives on life has always been salient. So to me at least, my story isn't about race but about seeing things from different perspectives and, I'd like to think, being a better person because of it." The views that Taica, Anise, Dean, and many other students in this book espouse highlight a distinct advantage that multiracial individuals may have. George Yancey and Richard Lewis Jr. point out that individuals of multiracial heritage are able to function comfortably in various racial communities, which helps them succeed in a multicultural society.[25]

Finally, for Lola Shannon, whose father is black and whose mother is white, her mixed-race identity is interconnected with her relationship to two cultures—those of Jamaica and Canada. Although Lola lives in Canada with her white mother, where she suffers among her peers under the oppression of difference, she is drawn to her faraway heritage and father in Jamaica. Frustrated that she cannot look like or fit in with her prejudiced schoolmates, Lola believes that her racial identity and beauty are, to a large extent, defined by her connection to Jamaica. She craves sexual affection to fill the emotional void left by her father, which ultimately backfires when she is raped. Her idyllic vision of Jamaica is eventually shattered when, following the death of her father and her introduction to feminism, her eyes open to the island's tradition of sexism and violence. She concludes her essay by expressing her understanding of the intersection of her backgrounds: "By looking at my life as a product of two ethnicities, I have learned about what ethnicity means to many people, and I have learned what it means to me. I know racism; I know how many mixed people choose to be black because it's easier. I know white people who prefer it that way too. I am reluctant to resign myself to one side or the other, which shows up in many aspects of myself. I am neither black nor white, but I can be both. The strongest ethnic ties I feel are to others with the same heritage."

A New Mestizaje?

The term *mestizaje*, a mixture of races, has been used in Latin America to refer to the fusion of races on that continent which has produced a new people who are a mix of European, indigenous, African, and more. Like this new people, multiracials must fuse a new identity. Like the *mestizaje* celebrated by the Mexican philosopher José Vasconselos in his famous work *La Raza Cosmica* (The Cosmic Race), multiracials are often viewed as a metaphor for a new world.[26] If a multiracial identity is a new form of *mestizaje*, then the anthropologist Peter Wade describes it most aptly: "I have proposed a view of mestizaje as multiple and with many meanings, among them the image of a mosaic, made up of different elements and processes, which can be manifest within the body and the family, as well as the nation. Seen in this way, mestizaje has spaces for many different possible elements, including black and indigenous ones, which are more than merely possible candidates for future mixture; it also implies processes of inclusion that go beyond mere rhetorical discourse."[27]

The students who have contributed to this book push the boundaries within their communities and thus open up spaces that offer new possibilities. We hope this collection of narratives moves beyond a narrow black/white binary of multiracial identity and instead elucidates the wide variety of multiracial experiences that includes the influences of culture, class, gender, space, sexual orientation, nations, and regions. A multiracial identity has taken hold, and forecasters expect that it will be an ongoing trend. These stories paint a portrait of the concerns and experiences inherent in this new identity. As they look toward the future, these students, too, wonder what this identity will bring. Will we continue to allow people to choose more than one category, or will we again force individuals into a singular racial identity? Chris Collado in "So, What Are You?" reflects on what his future children will face: "Having gone through the process myself, I know how difficult it can be at times to be comfortable in your own skin. My hope for them would be that they would be proud of their mixed racial heritage and choose not to pass for whatever race they most resemble physically. Ultimately it will be their journey, but I will give my insights if they ask. My broader hope for our society is that with the population of multiracial children growing, we will be able to accept people as belonging in more than one category." By sharing the stories of students who have written and reflected so thoughtfully about what their mixed identity means for their lives, we hope this book will help others on their journey.

Notes

1. Audrey Smedley, *Race in North America: Origins and Evolution of a Worldview* (Boulder: Westview Press, 2007), 332.
2. *African American Lives*, directed by Leslie Asako Gladsjo, Grahm Judd, Jesse Sweet, and Jack Youngelson, Thirteen WNET (New York: Kunhardt Productions, 2006).
3. *Hypodescent* refers to the automatic assigning of the children of people from mixed racial, ethnic, or socioeconomic backgrounds to the minority group.
4. *Loving v. Commonwealth of Virginia*, 388 U.S. 1 (1967).
5. Kim M. Williams, *Mark One or More: Civil Rights in Multiracial America* (Ann Arbor: University of Michigan Press, 2008).
6. Karen Downing, "Accessing the Literature," in *Multiracial America: A Resource Guide on the History and Literature of Interracial Issues*, ed. Karen Downing, Darlene Nichols, and Kelly Webster (Lanham, Md.: Scarecrow Press, 2005), 5–12.
7. David Parker and Miri Song, eds., *Rethinking "Mixed Race"* (Sterling, Va.: Pluto Press, 2001).
8. Maria P. P. Root, *The Multiracial Experience: Racial Borders as the New Frontier* (Thousand Oaks, Calif.: Sage Publications, 1996), xi.
9. Smedley, *Race in North America*, 6.
10. Tim Wise, *White Like Me: Reflections on Race from a Privileged Son* (Brooklyn: Soft Skull Press, 2005), ix.
11. Duncan Lindsey, *Child Poverty and Inequality: Securing a Better Future for America's Children* (New York: Oxford University Press, 2009).
12. Charles A. Gallagher, "Color-Blind Privilege: The Social and Political Functions of Erasing the Color Line in Post-Race America," *RGC Journal Special Edition on Privilege* 10, no. 4 (2003): 575–88.
13. Jennifer Lee and Frank D. Bean, "Reinventing the Color Line: Immigration and America's New Racial/Ethnic Divide," *Social Forces* 86, no. 2 (2007): 579.
14. Williams, *Mark One or More*.
15. Joel Perlmann and Mary C. Waters, *The New Race Question: How the Census Counts Multiracial Individuals* (New York: Russell Sage Foundation, 2005), 1.
16. Ibid., 2.
17. Kristen A. Renn, Mixed Race Students in College: The Ecology of Race, Identity, and Community on Campus (Albany: State University of New York Press, 2004); Kerry Ann Rockquemore and David L. Brunsma, Beyond Black: Biracial Identity in America (Thousand Oaks, Calif.: Sage Publications, 2002).
18. G. Reginald Daniel and Josef Manuel Casteneda-Liles, "Race, Multiraciality, and the Neoconservative Agenda," in *Mixed Messages: Multiracial Identities in the "Color-Blind" Era*, ed. D. L. Brunsma (Boulder: Lynne Rienner Publishers, 2006), 129–30.
19. Lee and Bean, "Reinventing the Color Line."
20. France Winddance Twine, "Brown-Skinned White Girls: Class, Culture, and the Construction of White Identity in Suburban Communities," *Gender, Place & Culture: A Journal of Feminist Geography* 3, no. 2 (1996): 205–24.

21. C. N. Le, "Multiracial Asian Americans: Social Class, Demographic, and Cultural Characteristics," in *Multiracial Americans and Social Class: The Influence of Social Class on Racial Identity*, ed. K. O. Korgen (New York: Routledge, 2010), 115–20; Yu Xie and Kimberly Goyette, "The Racial Identification of Biracial Children with One Asian Parent: Evidence from the 1990 Census," *Social Forces* 76 (2997): 547–70.

22. Kerry Ann Rockquemore, Tracey Lazloffy, and Julia Noveske, "It All Starts at Home: Racial Socialization in Multiracial Families," in Brunsma, *Mixed Messages*, 213.

23 Kerry Ann Rockquemore and Tracey Lazloffy, *Raising Biracial Children* (New York: Altamira Press, 2005).

24. Rockquemore and Brunsma, *Beyond Black*, 42.

25. George Yancey and Richard Lewis Jr., *Interracial Families: Current Concepts and Controversies* (New York: Routledge, 2009).

26. Jose Vasconselos, *La Raza Cosmica/The Cosmic Race* (Baltimore: John Hopkins University Press, 1997). This book, first published in 1925, is about the new race of people who are an "integral race, made up of the genius and the blood of all peoples and, for that reason, more capable of true brotherhood and of a truly universal vision" (18).

27. Peter Wade, "Rethinking Mestizaje: Ideology and Lived Experience," *Journal of Latin American Studies* 37 (2005): 254.

I

WHO AM I?

1

Ana Sofia De Brito Good Hair

The issue of race has always been a problem in my Cape Verdean family—and in my life. We constantly argue whether we're white or black. My dad says he stayed with my mom to *melhorar a raça*, or better his race, by lightening the color of his children, and I'd better not mess up his plan by bringing a black boy home. In my home country, being lighter is equated with having money, which is a process called *branqueamento*, where money makes you whiter and marrying lighter helps your race. Needless to say, he is proud of his light skin.

I had always wondered what my dad had against broad noses. As he realized in my late teenage years that my taste leaned toward black men, most of whom had the type of nose he despised, my dad would always advise me to think twice.

"I hope you know what you're doing," he said one night when we went out to dinner together. "What do you mean?" I had no clue what I was doing wrong. "You're destroying the race I helped create by marrying your mom. All my hard work will go to waste after you have a child with someone with a flat nose and nappy hair. You better start learning to do black people's hair!" he replied, laughing.

Destroying his race? I was not aware that I was the product of his "hard work" to make the Cape Verdean race lighter, with finer hair and a straighter nose. For years I had heard him say he "bettered his race," but I never truly believed he was serious. He would joke about my hypothetical future husband by saying he didn't want to hurt his hand when he patted the Brillo-pad hair of his grandchildren.

It wasn't until I heard his life story that I understood my dad's sensibilities. When I was a child, my father was very evasive about his own childhood. It wasn't until I was eighteen years old and away at college that I started to question him seriously about his past.

In 1965, at age three, my father left the Cape Verde Islands with his mother, father, and two youngest brothers and moved to the African country of Mozambique, another former Portuguese colony. My grandfather had been sent by the Portuguese government to serve as mayor of a village in the interior of the country that was quickly growing into a city. It was in Mozambique that my father's views about race were formed. As the Cape Verdean son of an official in the administration of a Portuguese colony, my father led a privileged life, living in a big house with great food and many servants.

All this changed, however, when he went away to a boarding school attended almost entirely by the children of white Portuguese settlers. My dad was neither Portuguese nor white, so he was constantly bullied, beaten up, made fun of, and humiliated. He never talks about this part of his life in Mozambique, but the bullying he suffered has had an irreversible effect on him. The fact that his skin was the color of tan sand made him stand out in a sea of white, and his broad nose did not help matters. At his boarding school in Mozambique, the whiter students called him "nigger" and other epithets, the very names he now calls people who are darker than him. The white children in Mozambique equated him with the darker-skinned natives, whom their parents had taught them to look down on as inferior. Although my dad returned to Cape Verde at age thirteen, his notion of blackness and whiteness had been radically changed, and he still carries the mindset of the bullied child. Had my dad's family stayed in Cape Verde, where color lines are blurred and there is no outright racism, I believe my dad would not be the way he is.

My mother was born and raised in the Cape Verde Islands, including Praia, a city where slaves were sent to be sold in the time of the slave trade. On the island of Santiago, where Praia is located, there are more Africans and Afro-descended Cape Verdeans than on any other island. At age ten, my mom moved from Fogo, a volcanic island with a bigger population of whiter Cape Verdeans, to Praia for schooling. My mother is the lightest in our family, and her thin, fine hair goes with the rest of her features. She has round dark eyes and a straight European-looking nose, the thin lips associated with being white, and a pale complexion that turns tan only in the summer months. My brother and I both inherited many of her features, but our noses differ. Mine is broader and his is straighter, on account of our having different dads. And even though we have similar features and complexions, we have different mindsets. We both identify strongly as

Cape Verdean; he, however, identifies with being white, whereas I identify with being black.

It gets complicated when my family talk about skin color. They believe that black is ugly, but so is being "too white"; our Cape Verdean color is just right. My father seems to place Cape Verdean people in the category of an entirely different race. The reality is that Cape Verdeans are mixed both culturally and racially and are many different shades.

Cape Verde is made up of ten islands off the west coast of Africa. The Portuguese colonized the uninhabited islands in the fifteenth century. Like other colonies, Cape Verde prospered from the transatlantic slave trade. Cape Verdean people were literally born out of the interactions between the Portuguese, Italians, Asian Indians, British, French, and African slaves. Among those who call themselves Cape Verdean are blonds with green eyes and those who are dark as ebony. In between you can find any shade and combination of features. Even within my own family, our skin hue, the texture of our hair, and our eye color vary from person to person.

Our Cape Verdean-ness became even more complicated when we tried to integrate ourselves into America. In 1996 my mom decided to move to the United States and bring my brother and me along. I was five and my brother was fifteen. My father had gone ahead a year earlier. My mom stayed behind for a year because of her career as the manager of a well-respected hotel and restaurant in the capital of Cape Verde. We led a very comfortable life before moving to America. My parents were well-off, we lived in a spacious house, and my brother and I went to private schools. Nonetheless, the educational opportunities that were offered in Cape Verde could never compare with those offered in the United States. That summer we packed our belongings, got on a spacious South African plane, and came to the United States.

Our immigrant story was not that of the "huddled masses" often perpetuated by the media. We had no reason to leave Cape Verde. Our extended family is well respected there, particularly my maternal grandparents, because my grandfather saved many lives during his medical career, and my grandmother helped thousands of women give birth. To this day, people ask me to thank my grandparents for their benevolence. My grandfather had worked himself up from nothing after his father died when he was fourteen, leaving his mother with thirteen young children. He became a nurse and later pursued a career in politics, in addition to his medical career. My paternal grandfather did the same. His mother was a black Cape Verdean prostitute, who was impregnated by a white Portuguese judge and bore my illegitimate grandfather. He was sent away to be taken care of by his godmother during the hard times of World War II, when there was famine in Cape Verde. He excelled at school, became a pharmacist technician, and later also pursued a political career in Mozambique, becoming a mayor. My grandparents instilled in their children a love and admiration for education, which was passed on to their grandchildren. When my father left for the United States and sent back news that he had found work, my mother decided to move to the States as well to keep our family intact, and for the sake of her children's education.

When we arrived at the airport in Boston, my mom shouted, "There he is!" I turned my head and spotted my dad. It had been a whole year since I'd last seen him, so I immediately began to run as fast as my little skinny legs could take me to his outstretched arms. *"Cuquinha,"* he whispered as he gave me a hug. That was my nickname—and it had been a whole year since I'd heard the word from his lips.

When we pulled up to our new home, I was very excited. I ran up the stairs, but as my dad opened the door, a wave of disappointment hit me. For some reason I was expecting something other than what I found. Our new home was a bachelor's apartment. My father lived there with a roommate; it was gray and cold and smelled like cigarettes. I hoped with all my heart that this wasn't our home; it was so much smaller than our old house. Unfortunately, this small duplex apartment has been our home for the past fifteen years. For the first three years there, I slept on a mattress on the floor of my parents' bedroom while we waited for Nelson, my dad's roommate, to leave. We watched the years go by, and the street began to change from white to black. As more Cape Verdean and Latino families moved to our street, more white people began to move out. The streets in our neighborhood also became less cared for, and violence increased. I watched all this through my window and from my balcony, since I've always felt uncomfortable being outside in my neighborhood.

Our first summer in the United States was a period of acclimation. Everything was still new and exciting, but limited. After six months of living here, we became undocumented after overstaying our tourist visas. Our family went from being relatively well-off to living on a tight budget. Cape Verdean currency did not translate well to American dollars. My father worked cleaning offices for a business in Providence, and my mother was unemployed. She spent her time helping me learn English so I could be enrolled in school in the upcoming fall. We spent hours every night practicing with flashcards. Because my mother was the only one in the family with any knowledge of English, she was the one who helped me learn my first words in this new language.

My elementary school was attended mostly by Cape Verdean children of all colors, who either had immigrated to the United States or were born here, some Latinos, African Americans, and a few whites. When I looked around, I saw familiar faces and heard a familiar language. I never had to answer the question "What are you?" In fact, until tenth grade I never thought of myself as a "minority." This changed, however, when I transferred from a violence-ridden, under-resourced public school to a private all-girls Quaker school attended primarily by white Jewish girls. Overnight I became not only a minority but, because of my mixed racial background, also "exotic" and very much the "other."

It was in this school that I first became aware of race relations and socioeconomic classes, and how the two are inexplicably intertwined. Until then I had never given much thought to my economic situation or race. I knew I wasn't rich, but even though my mom was a domestic servant and my dad worked in a factory during this time, we were able to go on vacations to Hawaii and Florida, so I deduced that we weren't poor either. I wasn't very conscious of the various racial heritages that made up my Cape Verdean self, nor did I care. But then, suddenly, my school peer group consisted of seemingly rich white kids almost completely ignorant of people unlike themselves. I recall my mom's advice to me on the first day at my new school: "Remember where you came from and don't let these rich kids make you think they're better than you. And also remember, you're not rich."

I definitely knew I was not rich. As an undocumented-immigrant transfer student into the tenth grade, I was offered a discounted tuition of only $5,000, though tuition was normally $19,000. My parents, however, could not afford to pay even $5,000 a year, as we lived from paycheck to paycheck and continually struggled to keep up with the bills they already had. I cried every day for three weeks after being notified that I had been accepted at the school, knowing I would never get to leave my public high school with its gang fights, rapes, and restrictive atmosphere. My salvation came from a Jewish family my mom worked for as a nanny and maid. They offered to pay my tuition for three years because they believed that any intelligent child deserved the same educational opportunities their son would have. For this I will be indebted to them for the rest of my life. They allowed me to become part of their family and made sure I took advantage of every educational opportunity presented to me.

My private high school solidified my identification with being black. I came to see that in this society I wasn't just Cape Verdean—I was black. My parents had told me I was a white Cape Verdean, but being in a majority-white school made me think maybe I wasn't white enough. I soon began to analyze my life in the United States through the same lens as most Americans, who saw my family and me as black. Ever since we moved to the States, my father had been complaining that he didn't receive any respect here. He used to complain often about how disrespectfully he was treated by white people. This was especially confusing for him, because he thought of himself as white too, and therefore one of them. So he chose to assume that his poor treatment was because of his immigrant status or his limited English and thick accent, which forced him to work in low-paying factory jobs. He was never willing to consider that as far as white people in this country were concerned, his tan skin meant that he was black.

My family has long been in denial that in America we are simply seen as black. It wasn't until I participated in a majority-white world every day at high school that I realized we were highly mistaken. I was not a white American and never would be. To people who didn't know what Cape Verdeans were, we were just another group of colored people.

The rest of the world aside, within my family I am considered white. From an early age, I saw the struggle of racial identification becoming a problem even within my U.S.-based Cape Verdean family. I remember the first time I felt I was better than my cousins because I was lighter. I was seven years old and my hair was down to my waist. I was standing in front of the mirror having my cousins detangle my hair when the "hair problem" reared its ugly head. My cousins always fought with each other over who would comb my hair, which was soft and curly and long—not "black" hair. My cousins and I had just come back from the beach, and all of us had washed and combed our hair. Mine was air-drying; theirs was being flat-ironed and pulled in every direction by their mother in order to make it straight. My young cousin asked her mother why my hair didn't need to be straightened like hers. "Because her hair is nice and is not kinky like yours," her mother replied with a sigh. I beamed. To me at age seven, those words meant I had won, that despite my African features I had one thing they didn't have—*cabelo bom*, or nicer hair—and therefore I was whiter. I was too young to understand fully how prized straight hair is within the Cape Verdean community, or that my hair being "whiter" made me less black.

Today I find myself wishing my hair were kinkier in order to qualify truly as "black."

My hair is curly and fine. I do not use chemicals to make it straight; all it needs is one good pass of the flat iron—just like a white girl's hair. Being able to walk out of the shower and let my hair air-dry into my hairstyle is a freedom that my black friends do not have. Because of my hair, the black community has identified me as not being truly black. Thus I have to prove to them that I am African, that I watch black movies and know what relaxing and perming are—that I, too, have experienced racism. It's a constant struggle for me to identify as black, and I wonder how many more years I will have to fight to amass sufficient cultural capital to be considered black by other blacks.

The privileges I supposedly receive in America because of my light skin have been detailed to me by my friends at college who are considerably darker than I. They say that white people will treat me with more respect because I am light-skinned; that if I straightened my hair more often, I could easily be taken for a "maybe" white girl; and that I will be able to get jobs a darker-skinned person will not. With each such "privilege," my separation from black people becomes increasingly clear.

When I have challenged the idea that my hair can determine the course of my life, my black college friends say, "Of course your hair matters! It's been proven by scientific research that when a black girl wears her hair straight to a job interview, then she is more likely to get hired than if she wears her hair natural." A dark-skinned Dominican friend said, "When I have my hair curly, I always get curious looks, but when I have my hair straight, I don't. Watch. Straighten your hair for one day and see the difference in the comments you get." So I decided to straighten my hair for one day and walk around campus to see what would happen. Sure enough, people came up to me asking to touch my hair, and I got lots of positive comments: "Oh my god! Your hair looks so pretty." "Your hair is so long!" "Can I touch it? Wow, it's so silky!" "I wish I had hair like yours." "You're even more exotic now. You should model!" All I could think was, "Damn, my friends were right." White standards of beauty had won; my straight hair got me more attention than my curly hair. The most dramatic difference I noticed was that white boys who had never paid attention to me gave me flirty smiles and talked to me. Not once while I was wearing my hair curly had white boys struck up a conversation with me on a non-academic topic. Despite all of the attention I get with straight hair, I still prefer my natural hairstyle, which I believe makes me appear more ethnic, more black.

I often ask myself, "If I'm not considered black, what does it mean to be black?" In my Rhode Island hometown, my ethnic and racial identities have never been questioned. I'm Cape Verdean, and so are my next-door neighbors. We consider Cape Verdean a separate race. But since I came to college, my racial identity has been ripped apart, and I have not yet been able to reassemble the pieces. The look of recognition in people's eyes at home when I tell them that I am Cape Verdean has been replaced with a look of confusion among people on campus. Few people at my college know what Cape Verdean people are or even where the small island nation is located. People often assume I'm Latina or "that mixed-race girl." Never black. Never African. And with my fine curly hair, light skin, and mixed European and African features, I can see how hard it must be for others to understand me in this polarized racial world. To them I am exotic.

I desperately cling to my Cape Verdean identity, which is like a piece of string slowly unraveling and threatening to snap. If it snaps, I fear my sense of self will be in complete disarray. I identify as black, but in the eyes of the world I am neither black nor white. When I try to affiliate with black student organizations at college, black students often don't know what to make of me. They say, "I don't know what you're doing here," implying that as a light-skinned girl, I don't know what it is to be truly black. They seem to consider themselves the arbiters of who is truly black, and I somehow get lost in the shuffle.

After three years at college, I still feel there is a divide between dark-skinned and light-skinned blacks, and between African Americans and Africans. Interestingly, I am African and I identify mostly with African American culture, yet I feel as if I'm not being taken seriously at black group events because of my light skin. This has pushed me to associate more on campus with Dominicans, who understand my racial mixture and suffer the same type of discrimination.

My conundrum often arises on the dating scene as well. When I told one black freshman boy I was from Cape Verde, he said to me, "I like light-skinned girls with curly hair. And you're different from black people. You're exotic." It's hard to figure out if a boy likes me for my light features, because I'm exotic, or because of who I am.

Although I have never had a strong preference for any particular type and have dated boys from various backgrounds and races, at college my preference has focused on men with darker skin. Someone once asked me, "Why do you only like black men?" This question irritates me; why aren't white people asked why they are attracted to other white people? Is there a law that says I must be attracted to others who look just like me?

It's so much easier for me to date men from Rhode Island than from my college, as the locals tend to be familiar with Cape Verdean people, culture, and food. They know what Cape Verde is and can locate it on a map, so I don't have to explain my heritage and can enter the relationship knowing they will understand where I am coming from. My former boyfriend was African American with Cape Verdean ancestry. He has what would be considered black features and was completely immersed in the black community.

When my parents heard I had a black boyfriend, they had different reactions. My mom was genuinely happy I had found someone I seemed to like. Her motto has always been "It's you that has to like him, not us, and it doesn't matter what his color is." My father, however, responded, "Another black person? I can see you're stuck with that category." But when he met my boyfriend, his reaction surprised me: "Oh, I thought he'd be darker. He's just like us. I like him." It seemed my new boyfriend passed the test because his skin was lighter than my previous boyfriend's. Surprisingly, my father actually acknowledged him and spoke English with him. My previous boyfriend had hardly received a hello or a handshake.

Black men at my college are interesting. They seem to consider the dark-skinned girls more authentically black, and my light skin becomes a negative in their eyes. I remember having a conversation with a dark-skinned black student one winter night about the use of the word "nigga" and whether I was "allowed" to use it. "You're too light-skinned and you can't use the word. You're almost too white. If you were to use it, it'd be as if a white person were to call me a nigger."

I tried to explain. "No it's not. That's crazy. I'm not white—I'm black! If I want to call you a 'nigga' like you do with your friends and how you sometimes address me, I can." He replied, "It's not the same. You don't understand how hurtful it seems coming out of your mouth." I pressed on, with tears streaming down my face. "Because I'm light-skinned? Because I'm a few shades lighter than you, it removes the fact that my family was also part of slavery, that my family was also discriminated against because of their skin color, that my family also has had racial problems with the world? When *IN ALL THAT* did we lose being black and become white instead?" He chuckled. "Aww, I made you cry. You don't get it. You're still light-skinned. And you just can't use the word 'nigga.' That's it." He ended the conversation and left, as he saw that I was getting increasingly upset.

I was angry. This conversation, in the end, was not about whether the word "nigga" should be used or not. I don't condone use of the word and I don't want to use it. But the fact that he was denying my right to use it because of my lighter skin made me feel like I was being discriminated against by my own people. How could he not see that my family and

I also experience discrimination? It seems that because of my light skin, I am blamed for the world's discrimination against other blacks' darker skin. It almost makes me want to heed my parents' advice and date a nice Cape Verdean boy who understands the struggle of finding an identity in America, instead of having to explain myself to every new boy I date. The "Who's blacker?" argument gets old quickly.

In America, I often feel I'm forced to choose whether I'm black or white or "other." I prefer to choose "other" because I'm neither black nor white, but being in between creates problems for others trying to classify me. So here in the United States I identify as black, which is the most comfortable category to fit myself into, but I constantly feel like the immigrant stepchild to black American culture.

To make up for the lack of recognition by my fellow black people, I tend to adopt my friends' accents and mannerisms and try to appear "more black." I've become a great actress in the role of black American. My accent changes from southern to midwestern to New Yorker, depending on where the person I'm talking to is from. I've learned to talk about black hair and leave my hair curly to keep from looking "too white." I stay out in the summer sun as much as possible in order to get a tan and appear "more black." I take classes in African American studies, where I often feel that comments from lighter-skinned and African students are delegitimized because we have not gone through the same experiences as the African American students. Once again, there is the divide between Us and Them.

By the end of college I'll be able to write a book called "How to Be Black in America," based on my experiences of learning how to fit in. Fortunately, I think I've won over most of the student body at college. I'm now seen as black, though some people are still surprised when I announce I'm in the NAACP or part of the Afro-American Association. I wish I didn't have to mount a campaign to win people over to the identity I have chosen, that I could just be Cape Verdean and be seen as what I am instead of trying to fit into the single category of being black.

Regrettably, my family's ideas about racial identity are less evolved than mine. I don't think they are racist in terms of color, but they are against what they see as the black mentality, based on stereotypes perpetuated by the media and the poverty-stricken environment we live in. My father doesn't want me to associate with black Americans, whom he views as lazy, stupid welfare users. He's always surprised when I bring home black boyfriends who are educated, but they are never good enough for him: "He's pretty educated...for a black boy." My family and I constantly fight over the way they address black Americans, but it's hard to change their way of thinking when they continue to see the effects of poverty on the black population. This makes it hard for me to explain to them how their words affect me and make me feel like the black sheep in our family.

It's hard to live in a world where fighting for what you want to be seen as is not supported by your family members, which is summed up in what my immediate family marked down for the census—brother: white; father: white/other; mother: other; me: black/other. It seems as if America has thoroughly confused us.

I will continue to state that I am black, despite being labeled a "nigger lover" by my family, being made fun of as the whitest person in a group of "truly black" people, and always having to fight to be accepted as black. Maybe someday these racial categories can be dissolved and I'll no longer have to choose.

After graduating from Dartmouth with a major in Latin America, Latino, and Caribbean studies and a minor in Lusophone studies, Ana Sofia spent two wonderful months in Brazil and now works in a clinical research setting. She looks forward to becoming a health care professional and serving low-income women and being a part of the women's health care field.

2

Chris Collado   "So, What Are You?"

"Are you black?" "I thought you were Mexican because you speak Spanish, right?" "So, what are you?" These are the types of questions I have answered my entire life. I used to get annoyed when people would ask me "What are you?" in a tone similar to one you might use to ask about a homemade Halloween costume. I have been mistaken for being black, Mexican, Italian, and, on one occasion, Greek. I even had an older woman once ask me, "Has anyone ever told you that you look like Pete Sampras?" I don't think I look anything like Pete Sampras. It can be so frustrating to have the very part of you that makes you unique ignored. For the longest time, I couldn't understand why people saw me as anything but biracial or, the more socially recognized term, "mixed." My dad is Afro-Cuban, meaning that he is a Cuban of African ancestry and basically looks black, and my mom is white, with a European cultural background.

Before I delve into the development of my own racial identity, I feel it would be helpful to describe myself and provide a little more information on my upbringing. I am the oldest of five children. I would describe myself as having a caramel or light brown complexion, dark brown eyes, and thick, curly black (or at least really dark brown) hair. My dad has a dark brown complexion, dark brown eyes, and short black hair. My mom has long, straight brown hair, blue eyes, and a very fair skin tone. As I mentioned, my entire life I have been mistaken for being from a number of different races. It was difficult for me to understand why it was so hard for people to grasp that I am mixed. Maybe people aren't familiar with the growing trend of multiracial children. I believe people are easily confused by unfamiliar physical characteristics or traits. For the longest time society, as reflected in job applications and census forms, has been conditioned to categorize people in one box. I always wondered why I had to be one thing, one race. It's funny—I have had friends, acquaintances, and relatives mention how I look like my dad or have a certain feature my mother has, but I don't really see it. I feel that I look like what the combination of my parents' features should look like. Why shouldn't I look a little like both?

When I was a child, race as it related to our family—more specifically, as it related to how I should identify myself—wasn't a topic of discussion in my house. In fact, I never really asked my parents about my race. My younger siblings proved to be more curious about their racial heritage, especially in light of the election of Barack Obama and the discussion about his racial background. Looking back on my life, I think the reason I didn't discuss race with my parents may have been because my experience, growing up as a mixed-race child, forced me to navigate issues my parents didn't have to deal with growing up in one-race households. My dad had the same physical characteristics as the rest of his family (dark skin, black hair), and the same cultural background (Cuban food, Spanish language). My mom likewise shared the physical characteristics of her parents (white skin). I didn't know if they could help me. It wasn't like these issues were altogether negative, but could they help me negotiate how I would iden-tify myself among different race groups? Clearly, in terms of a collective perception of racial differences in America, we have moved beyond our turbulent history of slavery, the civil rights movement, segregation, and Jim Crow laws. I grew up with an Afro-Cuban dad and a white mom who loved me; I had Cuban grandparents and a white grandmother who loved me. I had relatives along both racial lines that loved me and were impor-tant in my life. My parents didn't push me to identify myself with a certain race and for the most part allowed me to try to define myself. At least I think that was their intention. My understanding of being a product of an interracial relationship was a realization that developed internally as I began to understand race and to learn about the history of race relations in school.

Today I openly recognize myself as being a biracial or "mixed" person. But up until this point in my life, my racial identity was constantly chang-ing with my given environment. When I was a child, I only noticed that the color of my skin was halfway between the skin colors of my parents. At that age, race wasn't important but rather something I merely noticed; I didn't understand the connotations or stereotypes typically tied to race. The color of my skin was just that—the color of my skin.

From the time I was born until I was about four years old, I would spend most of the day at my paternal grandparents' house while my parents worked. In spending time with my grandparents, who were Cuban immigrants, I was inundated with Cuban culture. I recall my grandmother cooking Cuban dishes like *picadillo* and *frijoles negros* as my grandfather would walk about the house singing in Spanish. In many ways Spanish was my first language, or perhaps it would be more accurate to say "Spanglish" was my first language. In the time I spent with my grandparents, I came to use certain Spanish words rather than their English equivalents. For example, I used *leche* instead of "milk." I used *elefante* instead of "elephant." At such an early age, however, I wasn't aware of the idea of culture, and I was only slightly more aware of race. I remember being in preschool drawing pictures of my family with crayons. I recall one instance when a teacher asked me, "Why did you draw your mommy in pink?" At that time, I didn't understand her assumption that my parents must be of the same race. I would simply respond by saying, "My mommy isn't pink, she's peach." At that time, race was nothing but a color out of a crayon box to me. I was tan, my dad was brown, and my mom was peach. These colors did not correspond to racial identities, interracial relationships, or mixed heritages. My artistic sensibilities reflected not so much an awareness of my mixed racial identity but more the pragmatic realization that the color tan lies between brown and peach in the color spectrum. Looking back on it now, I understand the significance of demonstrating my awareness of racial difference at such a young age, because my classmates did not think about or demonstrate race in the same way. My classmates, whose parents were more than likely the same race, might not have been as aware of differences in skin color, or at least reflect it in the manner I did.

At different points early in my childhood, my family lived in New Jersey and southern California. Both of these communities had diverse populations which were represented in the schools I attended. This was particularly true when I lived in New Jersey. I had classmates who were of different racial backgrounds and ethnicities; the fact that there were many children of color made racial diversity the norm. I was aware of the fact that I had darker-colored skin, curly hair, and dark brown eyes, but I did not think much about it because everyone was a little different. There were kids with similar physical features to mine, but there were also kids with very different features. Racial difference, however, had no effect on whom I or others seemed to interact with. I always had friends of different races. By the time I had completed kindergarten, my understanding of race had evolved from the point of crayon box comparisons to physical characteristics, but I still didn't perceive myself in broader racial terms or in the social implications of being a certain race. I didn't feel different from my peers until I moved to the more homogenous suburbs in Ohio.

Right before I was about to enter the first grade, my family moved to Ohio because the company my dad worked for transferred him to their headquarters in Cincinnati. It was in Cincinnati that I came to better understand racial difference and the internal conflicts that would arise in forming my racial identity. In the past, I had lived in more racially and culturally diverse communities; now my community was a predominantly white, middle-class suburb. I still remember walking into the classroom on my first day at my new school and realizing that I was the only kid in my class who looked like me. It wasn't that I was fearful or that I felt uncomfortable; I just knew I was different. Over time I developed a nice group of friends, all of whom were white. My understanding of being different didn't have an impact on my relationships, but I clearly recall it being in the back of my mind. I was aware I looked different from my friends. I remember seeing old pictures of my grade school friends and me playing on the playground where I was the only brown face.

My first encounter with racism occurred when I was in the first or second grade. We were studying Dr. Martin Luther King Jr. and his accomplishments, and our class learned a song celebrating this civil rights pioneer and his ideals of equality, harmony, and brotherhood. As our class proceeded to sing, a white friend of mine who was sitting next to me started giggling. I remember him leaning over to ask me, "Why are we singing about some nigger?" Prior to this conversation I had never heard the word, and not really knowing what it meant, I giggled in agreement. Seeing as my friend had said it, I just thought the word to be some new comeback.

Later that night, my family decided to go to dinner. I remember being very anxious to get to our destination, and I was getting frustrated because my mother was delaying us. While my father, little brother, and I waited in the car, I blurted out, "Geez, why is mom being such a nigger?" I vividly remember seeing my father's face tense up in anger. He exploded, yelling that I should "never say that word," and asserted that he did not even call his own brothers that. From my father's anger and the degree of personal sentiment that the word stirred in him, I immediately understood it then to be a very "bad" word. I did not understand the racial undertones or history that came along with it. This situation proved to be an excellent example of a drawback to my family not really discussing race while I was growing up. I didn't intend to say something bad, and I was confused. It wasn't until I grew older and studied the impact of slavery and the Jim

Crow era on African Americans in the United States that I understood the hate this word carried.

In elementary school and through junior high school we were required to take Spanish class. I recall things coming very easily for me. Vocabulary came quickly because these were words I remembered hearing my grandparents use when I was younger. When we were required to do projects on Spanish-speaking countries, on more than one occasion I had the opportunity to learn about Cuba. I started to become more interested in my cultural background. I knew the colors of the Cuban flag, the country's major cities, prominent Cuban leaders, famous Cuban baseball players, and I learned all about the food I loved!

By the time I reached high school, I had started to develop a better understanding of my racial and cultural background. More important, I had grown accustomed to being the minority. I came into high school believing that I had qualities reflecting both of my parents, and so I wanted to represent both. I didn't want to be viewed as black alone, because I felt that by doing so I would be separating myself from my mother. Similarly, I did not want to be seen as white because I did not want to reject my father. Because of my appearance, it wasn't very likely people would view me as being white in any case. At the same time, my efforts to incorporate the Cuban cultural background into my racial identity proved to be even more problematic.

I attended a private Christian high school where students came from families of high socioeconomic backgrounds and where there were very few minorities. In fact, in my graduating class of 108, I was one of only eight minority students. My core group of friends was predominantly white. Only one of my good friends was black. Despite the fact that I was in the Spanish club and took honors Spanish as well as AP Spanish, I was still recognized by my peers as black. It wasn't because my friends and classmates were overtly racist by any means. In large part, the lack of diversity at my school made race designation simply about physical features. There were no other kids in my class who had a mixed racial background. Because of the fact that I was darker than the white kids, I was black. It didn't matter that my mother was white or that I took upper-level Spanish classes and showed a heightened proficiency in the language. People classified me in the way in which people in the United States for centuries have been classified: by skin color. While I felt a little typecast, I was old enough to know that relegating someone to a single race group was a societal norm. It was nothing personal.

Regardless of how I felt about my racial and cultural background in high school, I found that it was a lot easier to play the part I was given.

My decision in high school to ultimately identify as black definitely suppressed both my biracial and bicultural identity. When people asked me about my racial background, I would simply reply that I was black. By the end of junior high, I had started telling people that I was mixed, but in high school I took a major step backwards. I think that high school is just an awkward phase in life. No one wants to stand out; you just want to be "cool." In fact, among my friends, being black was viewed as being a great thing because of the stereotypes of black people having superior athletic abilities. Not that I was an unbelievable athlete. I found myself playing up or humoring most of the stereotypes that defined me as being black. I would make jokes to my friends that they had no "rhythm," or if I were to get by someone when we were playing football, I would say something like, "I was really going there. Must've been those old slave feet kicking in." I even started addressing my friends as "suh." I would do so mimicking the voice of Morgan Freeman's character, Hoke, from the film *Driving Miss Daisy*. In the summer, some of my friends would come back from vacation with a tan and would argue that they were darker than me. I would always respond by saying, "I'm tan year round!" I even started to get my hair braided into cornrows, mimicking the hairstyle of many popular black athletes at the time. I wasn't fully comfortable with this role, and looking back on it I am kind of embarrassed that I played the part, but I grew tired of trying to assert an identity that would never jibe with the "one or the other" mindset of my community. It seemed like in some ways, especially with regard to sports and athletic ability, being black was a lot "cooler" than being white.

I also found that upon assuming "black" identity, I was welcomed into the small black network of students in my school, despite the fact that I was, in the words of my mother, more "suburban white boy than hood." She was obviously referring to my style of clothing, which was more preppy, and my family's very comfortable lifestyle—a stark contrast to the hip-hop culture my friends and I appreciated at the time. Whenever my friends and I were in a largely white setting, my black friends would often joke with me that we were the "only brothas in the place." Not only did my predominantly white peer group think I was black; I was in a sense adopted into the black peer group in my school solely on account of my appearance, and not necessarily because of my racial background.

Although thus far I have painted my adoption of a black racial identity through jokes and slang, I gradually came to realize that being perceived as black also revealed harsh societal realities and had a direct and negative impact on my life. When I was a junior in high school, I developed a crush on a white girl in my class. She had previously asked me to a Sadie

Hawkins–type dance, and we had had a great time together. As prom quickly approached, I was excited by the prospect of perhaps going to another dance with her. With the prom only a couple of weeks away, I asked her if she wanted to go with me. Much to my excitement, she said yes. My happiness was short-lived, however; the next day, while I was chatting online with friends, she sent me an instant message saying that she could not go to the dance with me. Because of my relative shyness around girls and my not wanting to pry, I simply responded, "That's totally cool," and I never got an explanation as to why she could not go to the dance with me. I had to admit that her "out of the blue" rejection after agreeing to go with me and her lack of an explanation were hurtful and served as a strong blow to my confidence, like so many teenage romantic rejections, but I didn't initially identify this rejection as a result of my race.

Later that weekend I was hanging out with a close friend, and I explained the strange prom date situation. My rather outgoing and inquisitive white friend decided to call this girl to get a reason as to why she apparently "changed her mind," because he thought I was due a proper explanation. When he questioned her about my prom invitation, she explained to him what she had chosen not to tell me. She told my friend that she couldn't go to the prom with me because her father was upset that she was going to the dance with "a black guy." When my friend reminded her of the Sadie Hawkins dance, she explained that she had kept her father out of the loop. I remember being shocked, angered, and confused all at the same time. At this point in my life, I was not so naïve as to think that racism did not exist, but I never believed racism would directly affect me. I remember thinking, "My mom is white. She is a part of me. I mean, come on, I am as much white as I am black." I never told my parents why the girl couldn't go with me. I didn't know what they would think. I remember being upset for a couple of days but ultimately having a fun time with my new prom date, who was black.

This incident remains etched in my mind because it proved to be the first time racism actually had an impact on me. It still really hurts to think about it. I wondered what her father would have thought if I had expressed the fact that I was "mixed"—that I was at least part white. I soon realized that it probably would not have mattered. It was like the reinstitution of the "one-drop rule": "I am part black, therefore I am black." I would still simply be a mulatto.

In high school I was called a "nigger" for the first time. It wasn't a common occurrence. But whenever my sports teams would play our rival schools in rural or urban locations, I found that one way my opponents would try to get in my head was to attack my racial background. I could be either a "nigger" or an "Oreo" depending on whom and where we played. I did tend to take these racist comments less seriously because I knew it was more about affecting my performance on the field or court rather than pure hate speech. Being called a "nigger" would nevertheless anger me because of the history of hate the word carried.

Unlike the experiences of my black peers who must also have suffered racial slurs, I was denigrated by both whites and blacks. My white opponents would attack my black appearance, and my black opponents would try to delegitimize my claim to being black. Because I went to a private school and was part white, I got the impression that the black students from urban high schools didn't feel as though I knew about being black. Or even knew how to "be" black. An opponent once called me an "Oreo" and told me that my football team had only "one and a half" black players, hinting that perhaps I didn't have the athletic abilities black players were supposedly endowed with. To him, I was not black. As for those who thought I wasn't black enough or didn't think I knew about being black, I often wondered how the same people would handle the struggle of being "mixed."

Upon graduating from high school and enrolling at college, I discovered the campus community to be an environment conducive to openly presenting myself racially. College is typically a period in people's lives when they can take advantage of the opportunity to express themselves fully. I was no different. My college was much more diverse than my high school; I had students of different races in every one of my courses. During my freshman year I was drawn to a sociology seminar examining the racial identity development of multiracial adolescents. I went into the class hoping that I would be studying myself, and looking back on my experience, I do feel as though this class is largely responsible for the way I view myself today. We read books about people who had experienced being classified under the "one-drop rule," we learned about the developments in legislation regarding racial identification, and we also learned about the social structures that impact whether or not multiracial adolescents develop a multiracial identity. There would be periods in the class when we would read transcripts of interviews in which young racially mixed people would explain how they came to view themselves, and I would notice a lot of parallels with my own life and my struggle to develop a racial identity. This involved growing up in a homogenous community, being recognized as the race of the parent you most resemble physically, and my period of "passing" as another race.

A large percentage of the students enrolled in the course were of mixed racial backgrounds themselves. Even more encouraging were the discussions I was able to have with them. I met a woman who was equal parts Native American and black, but because she was dark-skinned, she was frequently simply viewed as black. In public she was often forced to neglect her particular cultural heritage. We bonded over this concept of "passing" as a single race in the eyes of our peers and compartmentalizing our racial and cultural backgrounds, things that made us unique. It proved to be easier to play black than biracial. In her community it was much easier to pass as being black because all of her friends were black, and she possessed many physical characteristics stereotypically assigned to black people despite having a lighter complexion.

Still, not all of the students I met on campus with mixed racial backgrounds wanted to have a dual racial identity. One of my teammates on the football team was biracial; his dad was black and his mom was white, but he simply identified himself as black. His parents were divorced, and he actually spent most of his time living with his white mother. So I was intrigued that he was so openly and easily able to assert himself as being black. He wasn't the only person I knew who took on a singular racial identity despite having parents of different races. The one common factor among all these students was that one of their parents was black and they looked black themselves. As opposed to having people say that they were black, like me, these students could look in the mirror and *see* they were black. I look in the mirror and I can see that I'm mixed, from my skin tone to my hair texture. What if I didn't have the appearance I do? What if I had dark skin like my father or white skin like my mother? Would I identify myself differently? Honestly, I probably would.

After recognizing the number of people who deal with this struggle and also learning that multiracial children are a growing population, I became more comfortable in my own skin. It became a lot easier to identify myself as being mixed. I became more patient when I was asked to explain my racial background because I now felt that it was worth the time to explain it. I would tell people I was mixed, that my dad is a black Cuban and my mom is white. I noticed that I was beginning to hang out with a diverse group of friends in college. I also continued to pursue my mastery of the Spanish language, becoming a Spanish minor with an emphasis on Hispanic literature. My friends at school understood that I was part Cuban, and that it was an important part of my identity. In my Spanish classes I was able to meet and become friends with other Cubans, Dominicans, and Puerto Ricans, many of whom even looked like me and shared a mixed racial heritage. Once again it was easier for me to explain myself and my racial identity when I was able to hear the experiences of others in the same position. Despite the fact that I didn't use Spanish in my daily life, my Spanish-language skills made me much more proud of my Cuban heritage. Thinking about it now, I admit that if I didn't know Spanish, or hadn't at least studied Spanish, I wouldn't value my Cuban cultural background. I am the only one of my siblings who truly showed an interest in Spanish and developed a strong base in the language. At college I became very proud of being biracial and bicultural.

Being the product of an interracial relationship, I believe, has played a significant role in my dating life and, more specifically, the girls that I have been interested in. My parents never made race an issue, so neither have I. In my eyes, my parents' interracial relationship served as a symbol of openness. They didn't let racial difference prevent them from loving each other, and therefore I wouldn't let racial difference prevent me from developing feelings for a person of another race. I feel as though coming from interracial parents provided me with a certain freedom that perhaps children of same-race parents might not have. I had seen firsthand a loving interracial relationship, and I had watched it succeed. Because race was not a prominent issue in my family, I didn't feel restricted as to who I could date. In fact, for the most part I found girls of all races equally attractive. If you were cute, you were cute, no matter what your skin color, hair color, eye color, or whatever.

Despite the fact that I did not perceive race to be an issue when it came to who I should date, looking back on my experiences in a predominantly white private school system, I recognize that race definitely was an issue. I didn't have much experience dating while growing up, in large part because I was particularly shy around members of the opposite sex. In junior high, when it first became "cool" to like girls and have a girlfriend, I felt the push from my peers to be interested in the few black girls in my grade. I recall bus rides to baseball games when my friends would be talking about who they liked and who they wanted to ask out. They would ask if I liked so-and-so and suggest that I ask her out. But in junior high it wasn't just my guy friends that tried to shape my interests but girls as well. Friends of the black girls would ask me if I liked such and such a black girl, or tell me that a particular black girl was interested in me.

As I entered high school, I found that more black girls expressed their interest in me than girls of any other racial background. I actually attended the majority of my high school dances with black girls, despite the fact that throughout my high school experience I found myself attracted to girls of different races. It seemed, however, that each year a new black girl developed a crush on me. As I mentioned earlier, I was shy and relatively quiet around girls; I was by no means Casanova. I became curious as to whether or not my school environment, which was not very diverse, had an impact on why black girls seemed interested in me. Working off the idea that it is natural to date your own race, I began to consider that perhaps these girls were attracted to me because of my race rather than my personality. Looking back now, I can understand the way in which my peers and the girls I attracted helped to reinforce the "black" identity I adopted throughout high school. I had assumed that if my peers thought that I should be interested in black girls, and if mostly black girls responded to me, then it was only natural for me to identify with the black community around me.

Ironically, my longest and strongest relationship has been with my current girlfriend, who is white. She has blond hair, blue eyes, and fair skin. We have been together for over four years, and I consider her one of my best friends. I find it ironic that the majority of the past four years have mirrored my experience at college, a period of self-discovery that fostered the development of my biracial identity. When we began dating, race was never an issue for either her or her family, with whom I developed a very good relationship. I didn't care that she was white and she didn't care that I wasn't. We were simply attracted to each other and really enjoyed being together. In fact, we didn't even address the fact that we were of different races/ethnicities until we had been dating for several months! She has understood the importance I have placed on my mixed racial heritage, and she has never viewed me as one race or the other. In many ways I also credit her with helping to strengthen my identity. Prior to meeting me, she was already fluent in Spanish and deeply interested in the Hispanic/Latino culture. Upon learning of my racial heritage, she became influential in helping me to reconnect with my Cuban roots by trying to get me to speak Spanish more frequently with her (which she wasn't very successful in accomplishing) and exciting my interest in cooking Cuban food. I am thankful that I have been able to grow closer to such an amazing person, and I am proud of the fact that we never perceived racial difference as an obstacle in developing our strong relationship.

After witnessing my parents' relationship, I didn't hold any of the stereotypes that often follow interracial couples, like being rejected by their families and communities. I understand that sometimes parents who are the same race might struggle with accepting their children's interracial relationships for a number of reasons: they might have more traditional/

prejudiced values, or it might just be something they have never had experience with and as a result feel uncomfortable. Have you seen a movie
with an interracial couple where race issues are not at the focal point of
the film? And if there is an interracial relationship, is it between a minority
and a white person or between two minorities? My experience has been
that it's much more common to see a black person dating a Hispanic than
a black person dating a white person in a film, or even a Hispanic dating
a white person in a film. But because of my parents' interracial relationship and the values they instilled in me and a growing sense of personal
freedom, in college I felt that I could pursue a relationship with anyone
regardless of her race.

Adjusting to my next phase in life, adulthood, I can't help but wonder
about the next generation of multiracial individuals, more specifically my
future multiracial children. Depending on whom I marry, the physical
characteristics of my kids can be uniquely different. Given my parents'
genes, I could possibly have kids with blue eyes, straight hair, and light,
maybe even white, skin. Or I could have kids with darker skin and a different hair texture from my own. My kids might look nothing like me in
terms of phenotype. Regardless of what my kids look like, however, I have
decided that I will take the time to explain their racial heritage. I would
like my kids to be more aware of race and race sensibilities than I was as a
child. But, like my parents did, I want to allow them to choose how they
identify themselves, both racially and culturally. Having gone through the
process myself, I know how difficult it can be at times to be comfortable
in your own skin. My hope for them would be that they would be proud of
their mixed racial heritage and choose not to pass for whatever race they
most resemble physically. Ultimately it will be their journey, but I will
give my insights if they ask. My broader hope for our society is that with
the population of multiracial children growing, we will be able to accept
people as belonging in more than one category. After all, the U.S. Census
form has been changed to allow people to check many different races.
I notice the same thing on some job applications I've seen. I'm hopeful
that my kids will be able to embrace their mixed racial background fully,
should they choose to do so, and that others will be able to recognize the
fact that they are mixed too.

My experience of constructing a racial identity was largely a social pre-
scription in the sense that the way I chose to identify myself was largely
based on my understanding of race and my environment. When I was
young and living in a more diverse community, race was nothing but
a color out of the crayon box. In my classroom there were children of

different colors, and there wasn't any value placed on differences between myself and my peers. As I got older, the concept of race carried more weight. Living in a much more homogenous community, I was quick to recognize how I was different. Even when I started to understand my racial and cultural background, I assumed the racial identity that was projected on me by my peers. Although this identity was based largely on racialized misconceptions and stereotypes, I still found myself willing to play the part because it was just easier to fit in. After attending college, however, and learning about how many biracial individuals have dealt with the same issues I have, I became much more accepting of my biracial and bicultural identity. In fact, I developed a certain level of pride for my mixed racial heritage and cultural background. My experiences growing up conveyed to me that trying to develop a racial identity is a very difficult process for biracial individuals because of the traditional categorization of race within American society based on the race you most resemble in the eyes of others.

With the rise in multiracial and multicultural children, questions about racial background as well as issues of social recognition, cultural conflict, and racial identity construction have become more relevant. The people of the United States elected as president Barack Obama, who shares a mixed racial and cultural background. At the same time, President Obama is commonly viewed and praised as being the first "black" American president, proof that society is still apt to essentialize multiracial people and to "box" them into one racial identity. Viewing President Obama as simply "the first black president" ignores his white mother and the fact that he was raised by a predominantly white family—that he is, in fact, our first multiracial and multicultural president! I, too, have struggled with trying to break out of the "what are you" box because, when I'm faced with the opportunity, my background necessitates that I check several boxes, something I have grown both comfortable with and proud to do.

Chris graduated from Dartmouth College, where he majored in sociology and was a member of the varsity football team. He and his wife currently reside in Arlington, Virginia, where he works in marketing for an international law firm.

3

Yuki Kondo-Shah   In My World 1 + 1 = 3

A Bangladeshi engineer and a Japanese interpreter marry and move to a Republican congressional district in the middle of the Arizona desert... Sounds like the opening line of a joke, right? Well, if this were a joke, then I'd be the punch line.

Whenever my parents and I walk together, be it on the busy sidewalks of London, in a chaotic market in Beijing, or along narrow pathways in Tokyo, the reaction from passing pedestrians is always the same. First, they scan my father, a lean man with dark skin, a mop of curly hair, and features that place him as coming from the Asian subcontinent. Next they look over my mother's strong build, *mochi* skin, and straight black hair cropped close to her ears. She is clearly East Asian. Lastly, there is me, a mixture of my Japanese and Bangladeshi parents, looking a bit like both but not quite like the sum of the whole.

The passerby does his calculations—it takes but a couple of seconds—and then, relishing the joy of solving an arithmetic problem, he lights up in understanding, equation solved: a mixed-race child, the sum of two parts. Except that, unlike a math equation where 1+1 = 2, mixed-race children don't come out equally. Half Japanese, half Bangladeshi, but not a whole anything. Add to that mixture a move to the United States at age seven, and the result is a whole lot of confusion. I'm twenty-five years old, and if you asked me to describe my racial identity—like one-quarter Bangladeshi, three-quarters Japanese—I couldn't do it. Where would my "American-ness" fit in?

People always have labels for others, neat little imaginary stickers that they attach to other people's foreheads to make it easier to understand where they fit in the world. Black, White, Asian, Hispanic, Old, Young,

Rich, Poor, Immigrant, American, Foreigner. It's an easy task when individuals appear to fit into those neat categories, like items scanned at a supermarket, but it doesn't work with multiracial people, who are hard to place in the usual categories. You can scan and then rescan, but it's hard to come up with an appropriate label. Maybe the curious few will ask "Where are you from?" or "What are you?" But what happens when the labels people stick on you don't fit your self-identity?

I've worn lots of labels in my life. Some with pride, some with discomfort, some without knowing the label was applied to me. I lived in Japan until I was seven (even though I was born in America...more on that later), when we moved to Arizona. When I was eighteen, I said good-bye to wide blue skies, Mars-like desert-scapes, and cacti. I traded in my T-shirts and shorts for puffy down jackets and long underwear to attend college in New Hampshire. Up to that time I had already worn lots of labels: *ha-fu*, the term for mixed-race Japanese people in Japan, and *gaijin*, which means "foreigner" in Japanese. Also new immigrant, Asian, biracial, Asian American.

This isn't a new story or an original narrative. Many people immigrate to the United States to start a new life and chase the American Dream, but my story was complicated in that my family didn't fit the usual labels. My father, an engineer by training, grew up as the oldest of eight children in a Muslim family in Bangladesh. He fought with his fellow countrymen for Bengali independence and took part in designing the national flag. He then worked as a civil engineer, designing buildings and bridges and developing infrastructure all over the Middle East and Southeast Asia. My mother was always an independent spirit. When she graduated from the Christian University in Japan, she looked around and found that all of her fellow classmates were married. Feeling restricted by the limited roles women enjoyed in Japanese society, she purchased a one-way ticket to the United States. After working briefly as a teaching assistant in California, she began her doctoral studies in cultural anthropology at Stanford University.

When my parents met on a train in Thailand almost thirty years ago, they probably never imagined the child they would have or the kind of world I would grow up in. Japan is a homogenous society, where 98 percent of the population is ethnically Japanese, and it's notorious for being a difficult place for foreigners to integrate into or gain citizenship. I recently read an article stating that 10 percent of marriages in Tokyo are international marriages—that is, between Japanese citizens and foreigners. That figure really took me by surprise. But walking around Tokyo in 2010, my mom and I did see many multicultural families with multiracial children—Japanese mothers with Brazilian fathers, a black mom with a Japanese dad. This was not common twenty years earlier. When I was born in 1984, citizenship laws in Japan discriminated against Japanese women, and only Japanese men could pass on their citizenship to their children. My pregnant mother realized that if I couldn't be a Japanese citizen, then I would be a Bangladeshi citizen through my dad. She felt that would not be ideal and made the decision to give birth to me in the United States. That's how a Japanese woman and a Bangladeshi man gave birth to an American citizen.

I was born in California but moved to Tokyo when I was three months old. My first memories are of spending time with my grandparents in Japan, playing with my peers in Japanese day care, and learning Japanese. We moved in next door to my mother's parents, so I was brought up with 100 percent Japanese influence. I attended Japanese day care, played with Japanese friends, and spoke only Japanese. Although I felt completely Japanese, my darker skin made me an outsider to my peers. I was called *kurokogepan*, or burnt black toast, because I did not look like the other children. Influenced by their parents, society, and the media, children learn at a young age how to categorize others. I wore the labels of "foreigner" and "outsider" but was too young to comprehend why. Since I didn't know myself as anything other than Japanese, I found those labels extremely hurtful. When I looked in the mirror, what I saw was a tan Japanese child, and I didn't understand why people would think of me as something different. Nevertheless, I had no trouble making friends and still keep in touch with friends in Japan. We played *mamagoto* (house) and *karuta* (cards), bathed at hot-spring resorts, and attended New Year ceremonies with my grandparents at the neighborhood Shinto shrine. It was a classic case of nurture over nature: I was Japanese and I didn't know anything else.

I spent most of my summers in rural Japan, camping in the mountains and playing with other biracial children at the international camp that my mom sent me to. The camp was in a small town of thirty thousand nestled in the Japan Alps in the Nagano prefecture, near the location of the 1998 Winter Olympic Games. My mother, always wanting distance from the nearest neighbors, built a lone log cabin on the side of the mountain. For one school year I walked down the mountain path and through the rice paddies to attend school. The school rules did not permit parents to give students a ride back and forth from school, and you had to be beyond a certain distance from the school to have permission to ride your bike.

Through summer thunderstorms and winter blizzards, students as young as six were instructed to walk to school in order to build strength and confidence. I loved going to school in the Japanese countryside, where we'd catch cicadas and observe morning glories for science projects and participate in *Obon* summer festivals to honor our ancestors.

In 1992 my mother decided it was time I learned English, since my father didn't speak any Japanese and I was unable to communicate with him. Although my mother was a professional interpreter, she grew tired of having to interpret between her family members. During a business trip to the Southwest, my parents decided that Arizona would be an ideal place to relocate the family. That was, by my childish standards, the end of my life as I knew it. I resented the move because I was taken away from my grandparents and friends, and I was horrified to find that I did not have the linguistic or cultural ability to fit in in America.

I was placed in English as a Second Language courses and "developmental first grade" at a public school in Arizona. My parents thought the "sink or swim" method was the best way for me to learn English, and so I was dropped without a lifejacket into American waters. The majority of my ESL classmates were Mexican American immigrants, and I felt that, with my skin color, most of my teachers and peers identified me as Mexican as well. Although I struggled to learn English, the Japanese education system had put me ahead in subjects like math and science, so by second grade I was able to join mainstream classrooms. At that point in my life I identified as strictly Japanese, and I missed Japan and resented my parents for the move to a new country where I did not have friends and couldn't understand the culture. My parents tell me that I would come home and ask questions like "Why do the American children raise their hands in class when they don't know the correct answer?" which reflected my confusion with a new education system. I had gotten used to the Confucian system in Japan, which emphasizes respect for elders, conforming to the group, and following directions. On Saturdays I attended a Japanese school in a neighboring city, where I could learn from government-approved Japanese textbooks and earn a middle school certificate—this symbolizing, at least to me, my Japanese-ness.

My U.S. teachers would ask us for "personal reflection" and how we "interpreted" reading passages. This was quite different from the Japanese form of pedagogy I was used to. Teachers and parents would comment on how polite and respectful I was. My mother still laughs at the memory of other children's parents asking her how she raised such a polite, respectful, well-behaved child. Apparently my politeness and good behavior made us stand out as foreigners. Teachers and parents who saw my mom picking me up from school would ask if I was adopted, as my mother and I looked so different that we didn't seem to belong together. This made me feel incredibly self-conscious.

I remember being teased for making grammatical mistakes and having a foreign accent, and I was embarrassed that I couldn't pronounce words the way my classmates did. It didn't help that friends who came over would comment that our house smelled like "curry" and that my parents spoke English with an accent. I spent the first couple of years in America feeling completely like a foreigner, counting the days until the summer break, when my mom would put me on a plane to visit my grandparents and friends in Japan. For me, going to Japan was going home to the country where I belonged and where I fit in. There I could tear off the labels of "foreigner" and "immigrant." Or so I thought.

As soon as I landed in Japan, the flight attendants looked at me and asked in broken English, "Where are you going?" I took great offense at this, as I was *Japanese* and should not have been treated as a foreigner! I would reply in fluent Japanese that I knew exactly where I was going. This was met every time with a surprised look and a condescending "Wow, your Japanese is really good for a foreigner." Of course, when this happens now, I smile and just keep moving on, but for an eight-year-old who was sensitive about where she belonged in the world, these comments compounded my sense of *not* belonging.

But the worst was yet to come. At get-togethers with my friends, I quickly learned that after a year abroad, I was hopelessly behind on the newest pop music, TV dramas, and youth culture. To my horror, I would sometimes forget phrases in Japanese, and words would flow out of my mouth in English. My friends would look puzzled, sigh under their breath, and envy my English language skills. As time went on, I found that I didn't fit into Japanese society anymore because I was "too American," but I didn't fit into American culture either because I was "too foreign." I had become someone without a home, and that was terribly isolating. The Japanese label I longed to stick on my forehead didn't match those being placed on me without my consent.

When I was a young child, my tan skin was a mark of difference, and I felt it was a curse. I felt anger toward my parents for depriving me of my country of origin, where I could feel a sense of unity and conformity. I felt that if I had just one background, life would be simpler, and I was obsessed with wanting a "pure" identity. I felt that if I were just American, then I wouldn't have problems. I see now that what I meant at that time was "If only I were white." As I came to understand my own racial identity through interactions with other groups, I wanted to learn the markers and culture of the most "successful" group. I longed to identify with the majority group wherever I was, but because of my physical characteristics, I didn't fit into either Japanese or American society. When I was in Japan, I felt an increasing culture gap, which made it easy for others to label me as a foreigner. In America, I attempted to learn the cultural cues that would help me succeed socially—a goal that would become very important to me during middle school and the early years of high school.

In seventh grade I switched to a private prep school. This school was academically competitive and provided me with an intellectual challenge, but the demographics were high income and almost all white. At first it was easy to make friends, but I had a hard time really connecting with my peers. Even though I was involved in student government, I found that the issues I cared about weren't necessarily what my peers considered important. In the beginning I tried to fit in by being overly materialistic and focusing on my exterior characteristics, and was frustrated that I did not meet Western standards of beauty. I also wasn't an ideal student, as I studied only topics I was already interested in. I did join the debate team, which became a perfect outlet for me to express myself. Debate opened my mind to philosophies that changed the way I looked at my classmates and what we studied in the classroom. Foucault's theories on normalization and Naomi Wolf's "beauty myth" challenged the way I perceived myself and my relationships with others. Traveling around the country to debate tournaments made me feel successful. I began to reorganize my priorities and became more interested in the pursuit of knowledge rather than consumerism or shallow relationships.

I have always been extremely close to my parents because there are only the three of us. During college, and even now that I am starting graduate school, I call my mother every day and tell her what's happening in my life. Some of my friends think it's overkill and wonder why I have so much to say to my parents. I am especially close to my mother, and maybe at first it was because she was my connection to Japan. My parents were stricter than the parents of my American friends, and they made sure that I followed the values I'd learned in Japan—politeness, respect for elders, and responsibility. Although I spent some of my childhood resenting that my parents were immigrants, I was also hyperprotective of them. For example, if a bank teller was impatient with my mother because of her accented English, I felt angry. During my senior year of high school, I was bullied by classmates who made prank calls to our house mocking my mother's accent, which really hurt.

When it came time to search for a college, I wanted a school that made diversity a priority. Coming from a high school that lacked diversity, I was looking for an environment where I could find role models and mentors. During my search I was in touch with the dean of Asian American students at the college I did ultimately attend, and was delighted to receive emails from the president of one of the student Asian American organizations. Once I arrived on campus, however, I changed my mind about participating in this organization, as I felt that joining it would put me in a narrow category, and it wasn't a label I was comfortable wearing. I felt that the numerous Asian American organizations didn't offer a community in which I could participate because they were very country specific: the Chinese Cultural Society or the Korean Students Association, for example. I felt that the East Asian students would doubt my authenticity if I showed up at one of their meetings because I didn't look fully Chinese or Japanese; and, sadly, because my dad hadn't taught me about South Asian culture, I was afraid of being called out as a fake or a poser if I tried to associate with the South Asians. As a prospective student, I had admired the diversity of student organizations and felt it was wonderful that so many diversity clubs and organizations existed at the school, but at the end of the day, I didn't feel that as a biracial Asian American I could find a space where I fit in and felt at home.

For obvious reasons, I'm 100 percent supportive of interracial relationships. Since I am the product of an interracial relationship, it would be difficult not to be in one myself. Fortunately, I have my parents' full support in terms of whom I choose to date. My mother is generally more modern about dating than my father, and I frequently seek her advice about romantic relationships. My dad is more old-school; although he is already worried that I am too old not to be married, he thinks dating is unnecessary. Being in an interracial and intercultural relationship, however, my parents are very accepting of men from any background. Many of my friends' parents would frown upon their bringing home a partner from a different background, and it's a relief to know that the racial background of my partner will never be an issue with mine.

I have always been attracted to multiracial men. Whether they are Japanese and Caucasian, African American and Caucasian, Native American and Mexican, I find both their physical characteristics and their multicultural background incredibly alluring. When I was younger and didn't know many other people who were multiracial, my attraction stemmed from a nearly desperate need to connect with others who might have had experiences like mine. I would sometimes incorrectly impose on others the idea that because they were also mixed-race, they would understand where I was coming from or that the relationship would somehow be easier. It was as if I believed a magical chain of common experiences connected all multiracial people. Clearly this was silly, but looking back on it now, I see that it was my way of trying to find relationships with people I thought were like me. I now recognize that just because a man and I are both multiracial, it doesn't necessarily mean that we have anything else in common.

I am especially flattered when multiracial men find me attractive. Asian American and Asian men generally do not pay attention to me. I can't really explain why, but it seems that I am simply not their target. That being said, it is difficult for me to admit, but my most serious relationships have all been with Caucasian men, and my most recent and most serious relationship is with a Caucasian man I met at Stanford. Nevertheless, I've always found myself frustrated by these men's lack of understanding about the minority experience in America. On the one hand, I think it is unfair to generalize that Caucasians can't understand the experiences of minorities, but on the other hand, I recall countless fights over a boyfriend's lack of understanding or lack of passion for the issues that I care about. I also am acutely aware of being the "different" one in a relationship and am wary of being in partnerships where my mixed background serves as fodder for an "interesting" conversation.

During my early experience working in Asian college admissions, I constantly feared being detected as a fraud; after all, I was not a *real* Asian because of my mixed background. I was afraid that my colleagues and, more important, the students and families I met in my work wouldn't be satisfied with my knowledge of Asian culture, history, and norms. I was supposed to represent Asia in the office and be the local expert on all things Asian, and I wondered if I was capable of this. So I faced my fear of being an incomplete Asian and started to learn more about the community. I began to study the history of various ethnic groups and pulled out *National Geographic* maps to test my geography. I found that I genuinely enjoyed this process and began to take real pride in identifying myself as an Asian American. While I spent most of my childhood being Japanese and my college years identifying as a mixed-race minority, I began my professional career as an Asian American. It was all part of a process of growing and feeling comfortable with my place in the world.

Growing up, I hadn't thought much about my Bangladeshi heritage. Because I grew up in Japan and America, I identified more with those cultures. I often questioned my father's lack of interest in teaching me his language and culture, particularly given his willingness to fight in the Bangladeshi war for independence. Why fight to protect your homeland's culture and language if not for your own children? I still feel a sense of "racial melancholia" when it comes to my Bangladeshi identity, and when I visit Bangladesh or interact with South Asians in the United States, I don't know the correct cultural gestures or things to say. I have tried to talk to my father about this, but he just jokes and says that it matters only that children speak their "mother tongue"—by which he means my mother's tongue. I'm always in trouble when friends ask me about Bangladesh, because to be honest, I don't know much about the place. While traveling with my family to Bangladesh in 2008, I was surrounded by people who looked like me and expected me to be able to communicate with them, but instead found me unable to utter a single word.

In my previous role as a college admissions officer, I read around 2,500 personal statements written by high school students who revealed their innermost thoughts in an attempt to gain a place in a highly selective school. Many of these essays were well crafted but lacking in creativity, but a few were so powerful and personal that I found myself haunted by the student's words for days. One such essay was written by a multiracial woman who told about her mixed-race background. She shared her most intimate thoughts about her identity—how she had reconciled her feelings about herself and the way the outside world perceived her. Perhaps her words spoke to me because I could empathize with her lack of confidence and identify with her predicament. We were trained as admissions professionals not to have personal bias or to be swayed by emotions, but her words struck a chord with me. She described an incident when a classmate mocked her background and she found herself upset and crying. After speaking with her mother, she realized that only she has the power to define who she is. She wrote: "I realized I had no right to be ashamed of who I was. I put my energy into mourning the cultures that were absent from my life instead of embracing the one that helped me become who I am. My other cultures are here. I see them every time I look in the mirror. But neither my ethnicity nor any other person can define me. I reserve that right for myself."

Her words were so powerful, and her level of understanding so mature and sophisticated for someone so young. I found myself wishing I had been able to think at that level at her age, and possibly have avoided much of the confusion I had faced. Looking back, however, I can see clearly that the period of my life that caused me confusion and pain also became the foundation for who I am. I have benefited from my international background and from being exposed to many countries and cultures when I was a young child. I have also been blessed by being a mixed-race person because my experience as a minority in America has made me more able to empathize with people's differences.

I recently began graduate school, and being in a new environment and meeting new people remind me of how my identity makes me stand out. Almost every day for the past two months I've gotten the comment "Your name sounds Japanese but you don't look Japanese." Nevertheless, for the first time in my adult life I have found a community of Japanese people who accept me and treat me like I am one of them. It's a very new feeling, and because I am polite and my mannerisms are Japanese, they sometimes jokingly say, "You're almost more Japanese than Japanese people!"

This new experience—being a graduate student, meeting new people who have new expectations about who they think I am, and getting oriented in a new environment—has brought up old memories of trying to fit in or carve out a space where I belong. I spent high school being acutely aware of being a minority but not knowing what to do about it. I spent college being proud of being a student of color and organizing communities around this shared experience, while also being fearful that I wasn't Asian enough to be accepted by other Asians. I spent my initial years as an admissions officer fearing that the community would not accept my credentials as an Asian American. But here at graduate school, I'm fully embracing my identity. I'm actually surprised by the ease with which I sign up for Asian American organizations that I would have shied away from as an undergrad. My definition of Asian American has become more sophisticated, and I know that there isn't just one common identity within this group. Most of all, I know that my experiences and my knowledge matter. I'm happy that my background and experiences give me access to many spaces and groups, and the acceptance I am now getting from others is the validation I've been seeking for so long from others and, most important, from myself.

Since graduating from Dartmouth College, Yuki has pursued intensive Mandarin training in Beijing through a Dartmouth fellowship and worked as an admissions officer at Stanford University. After completing her graduate education at Harvard, she recently joined the U.S. State Department as a Foreign Service officer and will go to Bolivia for her first post, where she will work with youth and the indigenous community on education and cultural exchanges.

4

Allison Bates   A Sort of Hybrid

I have always felt like an outsider. I have never once felt like I belonged to something or someone. Thinking of this has brought tears to my eyes many times. At every stage in my life so far, I have had to deal with my race and what it means to be both black and white. I have faced one test after another, and each time I have looked to my siblings and within myself to get through.

We never talked about race in my family. When I look back now, that seems strange, because race played such a powerful role in our everyday lives. I didn't even understand what race was until I was older. As I grew up, this inability to locate what I was experiencing led to a lot of confusion around my identity. In the neighborhoods where I lived, I could see white people and black people and brown people and yellow people, but I never placed my parents in those categories. I never saw my parents' race, and so my mother wasn't my "white" mom and my father wasn't my "black" dad until I was probably thirteen or fourteen. I remember emerging moments of awareness: "Oh, yeah, my mom's white, that's weird." I recall wondering as a five-year-old, while waiting at the bus stop in Los Angeles with my sister and my mom, why people looked at us funny. I knew they were talking about us. Then there were the questions from other kids: "Are you adopted?" "Is that your mom?" "Why don't you look like her?" Over time I became embarrassed and found that it was easier to say I was adopted than to explain to my fifth-grade classmates why my mom was in fact my "real" mom.

To this day, the most frequent place of identity discomfort has been the checkout line at the grocery store. The cashiers never realized that my mother and I were together, and there would always be this awkward moment when I would have to say, "Oh, I'm with her." In some strange way, these cashiers had it right: I was always "with" my mom, but in many respects I was never really part of her. For most of our lives we lived in the same world, and yet our worlds were completely separate. I am black and she is white. We share genes but not racial categories. We stand in lines together, but the people around us don't realize that we even know each other, much less that we're mother and daughter.

My multiracial identity thus has largely been constructed by the reactions of others while I stood in lines waiting for buses or checking out groceries, and by the inevitable introductions at my school's parent-teacher nights. I had to learn about the history and complexity of race before I could recognize my own place in its ever-evolving categories. I am still trying to carve out my own space, because for many mixed-race people, the space that describes our particular racial identity simply does not exist or is in a constant state of flux.

I often wonder if my mom ever grappled with how to check the "race box" when it came to the forms and documents she surely had to fill out for all of her kids. Which one did she choose: white, black, or other? Or did she write in something else? I don't really know the answer to these questions because I've never asked, which reveals a large gap in my understanding of how my mother sees herself in her own family. I have often felt foreign and out of place when I am with her side of the family, which leads me to wonder if my mother feels uncomfortable about being the only white person in our immediate and extended family. Even though I am technically half white, I don't feel it; I don't even know if I'm supposed to. I have no concept of what it must be like never really to have to be aware of your difference. I think that is because, as a society, we see whiteness as racelessness.

As I grew up and came to identify myself as black, as having and being a race, my mother sort of got left behind. To me she didn't have a race because she was white. When I was in high school, this changed, as I began to see my mother as white and therefore "other." I became intrigued by black history in America. I read Martin and Malcolm and Baldwin. I joined my high school "diversity club" and got involved in projects aimed at eliminating racism. I even helped coordinate my school assemblies that were geared toward highlighting and celebrating the civil rights movement. All this began to make me hyperaware of race and difference, so that I gradually began to notice my mother's whiteness much more than I ever had before. I often stereotyped her words and choices in the same way that I had so eagerly urged my classmates not to do. So over time, as I became black, my mother became white.

As I look back now, it's hard to know if this was mainly due to being a teenager and naturally not always seeing eye to eye with my mother, or if I had simply accepted fully that I was black and therefore would always be different from her. I do think that my being black and her being white made it easier for me to assume that our misunderstandings were related to our racial differences rather than our generational ones. As a mixed-race adolescent, I had all the normal challenges to navigate in the ever-changing mother-child relationship, *plus* the burden of understanding my own racial identity as a mixed-race woman perceived as black by the larger world—a challenge my mother was incapable of helping me resolve.

My mother is a part of me, and yet so totally separate and different from who I am. There is a connection missing; it's almost as if there is this person I know but don't feel related to. I don't identify at all with my mom (or my dad for that matter), which creates a strange dynamic. Lots of kids have difficulty relating to their parents, but this is different. There is no way my white mother can conceptualize what it's like to be a young black woman in society. In turn, I cannot conceptualize what it's like for her as a white woman married to a black man and having a bunch of mixed-race children. For both of us, then, I imagine there is a sense of mystery and even bewilderment at the thought that our races have created this space between us.

Sometimes I wonder if the alienation I experience in my relationship with my mom is similar to or reflective of the relationship she has with her mom. There is a separation between them, too, a distance and tension that is so obvious to me because I can recognize the longing and pain my mother feels toward her. It is telling that I really don't know much about my mom's past. She has created a series of mental pictures that I use to imagine what her own life was like before she had me. Strangely, there are no photos of her childhood, except for one of her in the third or fourth grade. Bright red hair frames her freckled face; she wears a flowered dress with a green collar that was made by her mother. I used to keep that four-by-four-inch photo taped inside my treasure chest, and every time I opened it, I would stare at the picture of that little girl who seemed so unfamiliar to me. I would look at her lips that failed to form a smile and those eyes that seemed to be focused on something else, and wonder what she was thinking. What was her life like? What did her lack of a smile say about her childhood? Looking back now, I realize that photo in many ways sums up my understanding of my mother as a young girl. Lonely, longing for a connection with her parents, finding solace in the animals she grew up around on the family farm, struggling to close the distance between her sister and two brothers, only to resign herself to the fact that she was too chubby or stupid or afraid to measure up to them.

My mother's disconnection from her own family only grew wider as she got older. Unlike her sister, she loved art, not math, she got C's rather than A's like her little brother, and she loved horses instead of the cattle her father eagerly tended for most of his life. So when she went away to Brazil to be a missionary and then moved to Los Angeles to go to nursing school but instead opened an art studio, she truly became an outsider in her own family, the one nobody liked to talk about. This legacy would be passed on to her children. Furthermore, I think that because she was an outsider in her own family, she could not protect her children from having that same feeling.

I think that when my mom married my dad, it was the last straw for her family. She went instantly from being considered weird to seeming crazy. How could a red-haired, freckled-faced lady from a small town in California marry a black man—and an African at that! My father's culture as much as his color must have sent my mother's family into utter shock, because my father isn't just a black man, he is BLACK. His skin is so dark that it would be almost impossible to distinguish the black hair on his head from the rest of his face if it weren't for the tiny curls protruding from his scalp. He also has a heavy accent so distinctive that the minute he opens his mouth in public, he is transformed from black man to foreigner.

I've always felt more like an outsider around my mom's family than if we were a group of strangers. Our cousins look like the kids you find in a J. C. Penney catalog. Their families are perfect on the outside: their parents have good jobs and they live in big beautiful homes. Grandma had pictures of the other grandchildren at the different stages of their lives on display in her front room, but only one picture of us; a group shot of us sitting on a couch with forced smiles on our faces was tucked back in the corner. Their pictures lined the bookshelf like a treasured journey through time, but where were we? Guests at my grandmother's house probably assumed that we were family friends or neighbor kids. She never had to acknowledge us outwardly, never had to claim us as her own. Maybe that made things a little bit easier for her, but it certainly did not for my mother.

I have only a few memories of my parents together. One that stands out is when they were trying to move us out of our cramped two-bedroom apartment and into a new house. We kids could not have been more thrilled, as we hated our apartment. The only place for us to play was the parking lot, where cars raced in and out and the cruel asphalt left bloodied bruises every time we fell. We all dreamt of living in our own home one day. We would each have our own room, and there would be a huge kitchen where my mom could cook dinner while we played in the grassy yard with the golden retriever we kids so desperately wanted. The moment finally arrived when my mother announced that she had found the perfect place for us to live and was ready to bring my father and all of us kids to see it. I believe that there are a few significant moments that shape our lives, and this was about to become one of them. My mom made us dress up in our fancy holiday outfits. My sister and I put on our big pink dresses with the purple bow in front, while my brother carefully slipped on his black suede shoes, which perfectly matched his pressed black suit, crisp white shirt, and tie. My parents also put on their best outfits. These were the nicest clothes we owned, and they came out only on major occasions. This was huge.

As we drove out of our run-down, crowded neighborhood, things finally seemed to be looking up for us. After about an hour, my mom told my dad to park in front of a modest yet beautiful brick home with a small yard. The realtor she was working with was not there yet, so my mother got out of the car and waited on the doorstep. The rest of us sat in the van, barely able to contain our excitement. I remember my dad's eyes because they were beaming with pride. This was going to be our house; it was affordable, lovely, and safe. The realtor arrived and met my mother on the doorstep, who then turned and gestured for us to come to her. We threw open the door and dashed toward her, our excitement and anticipation making us fly. We arrived at the door, ready to pounce in and claim our territory, when we all turned to look at the realtor's face.

"You know, I don't have the keys to the house," she said.

"But they are right there in your hand," my mother replied.

"These keys are not for you. I just can't give them to you, it would be unacceptable," she stuttered.

"But…" was all my mother could mutter as she lowered her head and stared at the concrete steps.

At the time I could not understand the significance of that moment. My parents had experienced blatant racism before, but this was the first time the entire family was part of it. We were all there in that moment, our inadequate group not worthy of living in such a place. My mother stood speechless, my father cursed in anger under his breath. We kids could sense that something was not right. The air seemed different, the excitement was gone, and it was almost as if an element of fear had set in. We had never seen our parents in that state, our mother so stunned she could not form a sentence, our father completely helpless with no room to negotiate. We all stood there motionless. My brother tugged on the bottom of my mother's dress. "Mama," he said as he pointed toward the door. "Mine. Mine room." My father scooped him up from the doorstep and headed to the car. My mother put us in the van, shut the door, and just as quickly as we had arrived, we were gone. No one spoke on the ride home. No music was played on the radio, and my mom did not play our signature car game of pointing out all the yellow cars that buzzed past us. We were a family shocked into silence. It was as if that skinny little lady with her pinstriped blazer and plum lipstick had taken her magic wand and rendered my family powerless, meaningless, and unworthy. It hurts every time I think about that day, knowing that my proud father was reduced to a babbling servant, unable to find the words to make that house door open, simply because we were an unacceptable combination of white and black.

I think that in many ways my parents did not know each other; their ideas and dreams were very different. My mom lay awake nights wondering how to feed four growing kids, while my dad was contemplating how to support an entire village back home. Being a mixed-race couple in 1980s Los Angeles was not easy. It was as if by being together they lost the higher status that would have been theirs had they been apart. I still do not know all the details surrounding their divorce, but one day my dad left, and it was over a decade before I saw him again. When my parents divorced, I was too young to understand what was going on. One minute my father was there and the next he was not. It was something we got used to quickly. I was so young that it soon became normal to me that my father was not around. We never really asked my mother what happened or where our dad went, and I'm not so sure she would have had an answer for us.

Things had not always been easy even when my dad was around, and once he was out of the picture, things became very difficult financially. My mother had not worked since my youngest sister was born, and finding work with four kids under the age of six was not easy. She had supplemented my father's income by occasionally selling some of her crafts. My mom would later tell us that he often went overseas for weeks at a time, making business deals and visiting family, and he often did not leave my mom with enough money to get by. So she had created her own bag of tricks. She made crafts to sell on the corner outside our apartment and made a lot of our clothes in order to save money, and sold some of the clothes she made as well.

We were always dependent on the generosity of other people to get by. As hard as my mom tried, without a college education there was just no way she could make enough money to house, clothe, and feed five people. So one day she packed up what would fit in the back of our van and headed off to live with her parents, who were settled in a nice suburb right outside Sacramento, California. My grandparents had a house with three bedrooms, and we took over two of them and then some. It went from being a nice spacious place to a cramped living environment, but it was still the nicest house and neighborhood we had ever lived in. We lived there for about a year while my mother went back to school to get her nursing certificate. I think our presence shocked the quiet white neighborhood. We always felt we were different because we were poor and our parents weren't together, but my mom never talked to us about race. I don't know if she chose not to because she was trying to protect us, or whether she was just not aware of how deeply it would impact us. The confusion only deepened when my mother remarried.

My mother and siblings and I had moved out of my grandmother's house and were living in a moss-green duplex with a mulberry tree out front. We were all sitting around the kitchen table, and the morning sun beaming through the windows created a sepia effect. We were eating cereal when my mom announced to the four of us that she was getting remarried. I was so stunned that I dropped my metal spoon onto the linoleum. I can still recall the clang it made as it hit the floor, and it still makes my skin crawl. I was reacting less to the fact that my mother was getting married than to the man she was going to marry, Lenny. I despised him. He was mean and scary and incredibly intimidating.

Lenny was my stepdad for eight long, exhausting years that I would like to forget. I have tried to bury all recollection of that period and have so deeply repressed those memories that even now I'm startled when I recall that part of my life. We never speak about Lenny. In fact, his name is almost like a curse word. Lenny was old. His skin was tight and rough and covered in so many tattoos that he didn't look so much white as green. He had red hair scattered across his arms and legs and wore big yellow glasses with lenses so thick that it looked like his eyeballs were protruding from their sockets. Before we came into Lenny's life, he had fathered numerous children and had even more criminal convictions. He was prone to cursing and farting and burping out loud. I just found him, well, nasty. And I think this nastiness extended to the way he treated my siblings and me. He did not care for us and it showed. He went out of his way not to show up at our school or sporting functions. He derided us for making simple mistakes, and whenever he addressed my mother about us, it was always "your daughter" or "your kids." The few daily interactions we had consisted of him yelling at us and then marching off to the garage, where he would lock himself up for the night. It was a terrible and sometimes terrifying way to live.

Lenny was one of the few adult white men I had met up to that point. Therefore, I often associated his behavior with that of all white people. Looking back, I wonder if part of his obvious contempt for us had to do with our being black. On the few occasions we went out together as a family, it was always awkward. I mean, here were these four little black kids with these white adults, so the natural assumption was that either they were our neighbors taking us out for a meal or they had graciously adopted us. As a mixed-race child and a young woman trying to navigate a racialized world, I always felt out of place in that situation—feelings of displacement and disruption that would come to permeate my life.

My mother finally divorced Lenny and our family moved away, hoping to leave those bad memories behind. We next settled in a small town in western Washington State. My mom had a friend who let us live in a small trailer sitting in the driveway. The trailer was so tiny that we had to turn the bathtub into a sleeping area for my youngest sister. I remember how horrified I was at living in a trailer in the front yard of a beautiful home in a fancy neighborhood. I could imagine people thinking, "Look at those poor blacks who cannot afford a home." One of the worst moments was when the girl next door, who was the same age as me, pulled her brand-new BMW into the driveway as we emerged from the tattered trailer with our laundry. She took off her sunglasses and looked us up and down in disgust. I would later run into her again, in class.

I wound up attending a high school that was predominantly middle-class white and had immense resources. I struggled with making new friends because I resented the sense of privilege and entitlement of many of my peers. And while I became very involved in activities such as volleyball and diversity club, I always felt like an outsider, as though I was watching everything going on around me in slow motion. In spite of these obstacles I excelled, in part because I was determined to overcome the difficulties of my youth, but primarily because I had a couple of outstanding teachers who believed in my ability to change things for the better. They were the ones who introduced me to the meaning and value of education and encouraged me to apply to college.

In order to understand the person I am and will become, one has to understand the relationship I have with my father. He is as temperamental and cruel as he is friendly and smart. He is a controversial figure, one who is difficult to define and get to know. My dad came back into our lives again when I was seventeen. Only now, at age twenty-two, am I really getting to know him. One day at the beginning of my junior year in high school, my mother announced that my father was coming from California to visit us. We were all shocked because we had not seen him since we were little kids and had spoken to him only a few times on the phone since then. So one day he showed up and he hasn't left since. Neither he nor my mother ever explained to us that he was staying permanently. They also never mentioned anything about getting remarried, but I came home from school one day to find they had gotten married again. They never communicated anything to us.

I had never really known my father. When he returned, my siblings and I were nearly adults, so we did not need or want this man who had abandoned us to be our live-in father again. His presence was the ultimate clash in cultures, and our home life became increasingly tense with each passing day. I had become so used to being the second breadwinner in the family that I resented his authority. I worked two jobs and bought a car. I took my siblings to school and to their afterschool activities and picked them up. I got the groceries and helped everyone with their homework. I had essentially assumed a role this man was now trying to take back, although he had done nothing to earn it.

My father is a complex man. He has been in the United States longer than he lived in his native Ghana, yet he is still a stranger here, an outsider. The tribal scars on his face are embedded deep in his cheeks, a holding place for the pain of his past. He is ebony black and stands out in the daylight like an eyesore, so he can't be missed. When evening approaches, he fades into the colors of the night sky, his face disappearing. Only the round whites of his eyes stand out like glowing lights. His eyes, too, are dark; there is no distinction between his iris, pupil, and retina, and they seem to merge into one dark circle. His hair is as black as his skin; only the aging gray strands stand out. His three oldest children tower over him. Even without ever seeing my father, you would know he is a foreigner by his heavy accent. He can be kind, and is actually quite friendly and outgoing. In fact, one of the things I admire most about him is his ability and willingness to talk to or befriend anyone. But we are still so different from him and look nothing like him, and it is hard to believe we are his kids. The only thing that ties us to him in public is that we all are black.

My siblings and I had grown up black. We were black American kids, not African or Ghanaian. We lived in black neighborhoods and went to black schools. Black people did our hair, and we went to a black church. There was nothing African about us. My father was born and raised in Ghana. He came to the United States when he was in his late twenties, but he never really settled down here and often took trips back home. He is still not a U.S. citizen. Like many Africans, he has a negative view of blacks in America, a view he soon began to project onto us, his "black" children. He felt that we were too lazy, that we did not study long enough or work hard enough. Nothing we did was ever good enough for him. It was as if he was trying to strip that black identity away from us and turn us into the West African children he never had. One of the ways he tried to do this was to send us to a Ghanaian church. During the service they did not speak one word of English. Every song, sermon, and statement was in the Ghanaian language of Twi-Fante. All of us—especially my mother, who was the only white woman in the building—felt like complete outsiders. We had no real business being there, and everyone seemed to know it except my father. We continued to have clashes with him, but once he saw how successful we had become and how well we were doing in school and athletics, he backed off a little and slowly began to embrace us. It would take several more years, however, before we began to embrace him, even in a small way.

I was in Los Angeles when I received notice of my acceptance to college. My twin sister was accepted to the same college, and so we shared the experience. I had no expectations because I had never been to New England and was unfamiliar with the school. When I arrived on campus, I dove right into my classes and many of the activities going on around me. I even joined the rugby team. I became a history major and joined the business club. I went on service trips to New Orleans and Washington, D.C. And yet I also found my college incredibly isolating at times. It is an elite institution, and the individuals who wield power here are white men, and though not always noticeable, these characteristics permeate the culture and create a climate that is often intolerable.

My fascination with Africa started when I was five or six. Whenever my father's relatives came around or my family went to the homes of my dad's friends or to church functions, I would stare at the women in their magnificently colorful head wraps and scarves. I would listen to them speak, yearning to know what was being said. These people were strange and unfamiliar to me, and yet I was captivated by their culture—which in many ways was supposed to be mine but, sadly, was not. The smells of *fuw fuw* and fried plantain were as much a part of my early childhood as chicken fritters and pizza. These smells and sights and sounds helped me to frame a wider picture of what Africa must be like. At these gatherings I felt connected and yet disconnected, but I always paid attention to every detail, meticulously recounting names and faces. And this was how I came to imagine Africa.

When I got older and began learning about African history and society, I often felt confused. The images and stories of abject poverty and disease, of scandal, corruption, and sheer desperation were directly counter to my initial experiences and understanding of the continent. Surely the people I had encountered and the joy for life they exhibited could not have been born in a place filled with such melancholy. There was a conflict between the Africa I had experienced and the Africa in my textbooks and on TV. My experiences as a child framed my understanding and, later, my passion for the continent.

I realize now that this intense interest was rooted in something much deeper: my desire to know my father. My dad left my family when I was very young, and the things that I knew about him and the memories I had were very limited. Therefore my desire to learn about the continent and to travel there stemmed from a profound longing to settle my feelings toward my father and my own racial identity. I thought if I could just go to Africa I would have some sort of revelation that would free me from the questions and self-doubts that I held inside. In many ways, Africa served as a fantasy destination to which I dreamed of escaping to get away from all of my problems. I was attempting to locate the misplaced fragments of my identity.

Growing up mixed-race, I grappled not only with having a white mother but also—and probably more significantly—with attempting to figure out where my hybrid nature fit into the black/white binary of America's racial categorization. Particularly while in high school, I struggled with whether I was "black enough" or if I was really African American, since I could not trace my black lineage back to slavery. These musings were only compounded by my experiences of marginalization and subjugation. I say all of this to provide a backdrop for understanding how incredibly meaningful it was for me when I actually got to go to Africa during college. I earned a traveling grant from my college, which made the trip possible.

The first thing I remember when my twin sister and I stepped off the plane in Accra, Ghana, was the way the hot air stuck to my skin like molasses. This feeling would permeate the trip, and I never became comfortable with it. As my sister and I walked across the airport tarmac, we looked at each other and smiled. We had arrived. Over a lifetime I had built up so many vague expectations about what I would learn about myself from traveling to Africa. What I discovered primarily is that it's rather hard to find something if you don't know what exactly you're looking for, but it eventually occurred to me that this was not the end of my search or the fulfillment of a dream. This was a beginning.

Any delusions I had about not being culture-shocked soon dissipated. I was often reminded of my outsider status during my three-month stay in Ghana. I was constantly reminded that, in the eyes of Ghanaians, I would never be one of them. I found that it was not my status as an American but my skin color that made me stand out. I came to realize that being perceived as a racial other was nearly impossible to escape, even in the country of my father's birth. Wherever we went in Ghana, people would shout *obroni*, which roughly translates to "white person." Even the children at the orphanage where we worked refused to call us by our names and instead always called us *obroni*. I remember thinking, "I went halfway around the world back to my black roots, only to be called a *white girl.*" This was the most frustrating aspect of being in Ghana—more frustrating than the bucket showers and the endless traffic and the merciless mosquitoes. It hurt even though it was not meant to, because I felt that I was being rejected and that my identity was more confused and wounded than ever. My entire life up to that point had been a series of internal struggles between black and white, between multiracial and raceless, between African and American. I learned that the racial concepts of "mixed" and "bi-" and "multi-" are just as unfamiliar in Ghana as they are in America. As always, I felt out of place.

I realize now that all those feelings were inevitable. After all, I did not speak the language fluently, I found much of the food to be unpleasant, and I was constantly harassed for money and dates and photos. All the hopes and dreams of my childhood had raised my expectations to an impossible level. I came to realize that part of my desire to go to Ghana came from an incessant need to belong and be accepted, to have my differences be the norm. Instead, being in Ghana only confirmed my abnormality. I was initially very disappointed and upset, as I hadn't anticipated that my racial status as a sort of hybrid would be such a big deal.

My trip to Africa highlighted a bizarre dichotomy: I was black in America and white in Africa. I was always one or the other; nowhere was I both. Moreover, I did not like being seen as a white person in Africa because I understood some of the connotations and historical associations that came with that. And whereas I was considered poor in the United States, I was privileged in Ghana. Where I had been marginalized at home, I now became powerful. All of this was confusing and unfamiliar to me.

While my struggles with the way I was racially identified were certainly palpable, they did not define my experience or hinder my ability to explore and enjoy my surroundings during my three months in Africa. I went to soccer matches in Accra, traveled to fish markets in Tema, explored the forests of Kumasi, walked through slave castles in Cape Coast, and met, for the first time, my father's relatives in the village of Mim. Traveling to my father's village stands as a powerful moment in my life because I began to see why my father is the way he is. By rooting myself in his culture, I uprooted my previous misconceptions about who he was. I came to see him in the shopkeepers, government officials, and taxi drivers I encountered. Witty and smart and driven—these were the qualities my father shared with his countrymen. Meeting his family—my family—for the first time was a startling experience. I was amazed and moved to see how much my twin sister and I looked like our great aunt. For the first time in my life I was able to look at members of my extended family and see myself. What we didn't share in language we made up for in gestures and facial expressions and unspoken understanding. For the first time I felt at ease and had a sense of belonging.

The trip to Africa was an important part of my college experience and my evolving identity. It's fair to say that my college years transformed my identity. I became much more self-aware and sure of myself. But I also struggled to navigate the narrow lines between my race, my gender, and my social class. To deal with these conflicts more effectively, I became involved with the Afro-American Society, which became both a haven and a source of immense tension for all the reasons implicit in my story. As I prepare to graduate from college, I do so with an appreciation for what I've learned and how far I've come. I have been shaped by the people I've met and by the places I have gone. I carry with me the transformative experiences and the insights gained from challenges I have worked hard to overcome. I have learned these lessons from both my mistakes and my victories, and will surely carry them with me for a lifetime.

Allison moved back to California after Dartmouth to work for a large tech company for several years. She is now working for one of the fastest-growing start-ups in Silicon Valley and establishing a career in the world of technology.

II

IN-BETWEENNESS

5

Shannon Joyce Prince Seeking to Be Whole

A particular memory from my teenage years stands out as one experience that shaped how I thought about race, racism, and responsibility. Ironically, it's a memory of the extremes a white woman took to make my family feel welcome in a predominantly white space. We were at the Greenbrier in White Sulphur Springs, West Virginia, a centuries-old resort staffed by many black employees, where my family and our friends are usually the only nonwhite patrons. A docent was explaining some of the resort's history to us, and she pointed to a lithograph of the resort from back in the 1700s.

"You see," she said, beaming at my little sister Ashley and me, "if we were back in the colonial era, the two of you young ladies would be sitting on the porch drinking tea." My sister and I both tried desperately not to laugh. We knew that we definitely would not have been drinking tea on the porch of the Greenbrier in the 1700s. But the docent was so unwilling to face the human rights abuses of the past—and the inequity of the present that still kept most nonwhites out of the Greenbrier, except as staff—that she, wittingly or unwittingly, engaged in historical revisionism. She completely lied.

That revisionism couldn't help but throw some light on the truths I hadn't been able to see before. The experience was compounded on that same trip when an African American bellman smiled at Ashley and me and asked, "Is everyone treating you well?"

"Oh, yes," we told him. "Everyone has treated us beautifully."

"I know they have," he said, and then his smile became more conspiratorial, "because we take care of our own." Even though I'm a mix of cultures, three of which the bellman probably wouldn't consider "his own," the way I experience race means that all of me feels a sense of solidarity with someone offering good-natured kinship. I realized the bellman was articulating the attitude of many nonwhite service workers I had encountered, especially those at my predominantly white, private college preparatory school. They encouraged and supported us, their pride always evident. They did take care of their own, but what about us? I realized that minority individuals privileged enough to benefit from institutions like private schools or historic resorts had responsibilities to those men and women not given the same opportunities. The fact that in both contexts white people got to be the students and guests while nonwhite people were stuck with the brooms and frying pans wasn't an accident. It was an inequity. It was the direct result of the situation the docent had been too uncomfortable to acknowledge. My experience at the Greenbrier occurred when I was a teenager, but if I'm going to describe my journey with race, I'll need to go back much further.

Whenever I've been called on to define my heritage, I've never been perplexed about how to answer. My response has not changed since I was first able to speak, just as my ethnic identity has never shifted. When asked what I am, I smile and say, "I am African American, Cherokee (Aniyunwiya) Native American, Chinese (Cantonese) American, and English American." I excise nothing of myself. I claim the slave who was a mathematical genius; the storyteller, the quilt maker, and the wise healer; the bilingual railroad laborer and the farmer—regardless of the amount of melanin in any of their skins. I pay no attention to the pseudoscientific idea of blood quantum (the idea that race is a biological, measurable reality) and am uninterested in dividing myself into fractions. I am completely, concurrently, and proudly all of my heritages.

From the time I was able to think about such things, I have considered myself both quadricultural and ana-racial (my personal neologism for "without race.") I am zero (raceless) and hoop (part of peoples from all over the world). I think my parents might have been a little more comfortable with my homogenous white world had I been a little less comfortable in it, but I felt that four peoples had found space in my blood; thus, people of all bloods belonged in every space in general. I was comfortable at school not because I didn't know who I was but because I did. And I knew who I was because I came from a strong family.

When I was little, I didn't recognize my relationships with my relatives as being racialized. I adored and was close friends with my black/white/Cherokee great-grandfather, Papa, but it was my African American great-grandmother, Mamo Seal, whom I idolized. I was able to bond with Papa. With his gold skin, straight hair, and pale blue eyes that other nonwhites had been trained to worship, Papa was my playmate. We drove tractors together, walked through the woods, and played with the cows on his farm. I recognized that his startling azure eyes made him unique, and I admired his uniqueness, but I didn't value his irises over any others. In contrast, Mamo Seal inspired genuflection. To me, my African American great-grandmother was and remains an unparalleled beauty. Her most celebrated quality was her dark skin—hence her name. She was a feisty woman not entirely opposed to profanity. I usually sat across the room from her, not in her lap, and listened to her rather than chatting with her.

One of my fondest memories is of helping her to dress. I remember guiding a bright scarlet dress over her head, ringing her neck with crayon-bright glass beads, pulling stockings over her ebony calves, wondering if the baby-soft texture of her skin was somehow connected to its pure blackness. The world tried to teach me to see beauty as Papa, but Papa saw beauty as Mamo Seal, and so did I. When I was young, Mamo Seal (and Papa, too) were simply beautiful. As I grew older, their beauty was politicized. And in a world where Queen Elizabeth was on the curriculum but not Yaa Asantewaa, where girls dreamed of being Britney Spears but not India Arie, seeing Mamo Seal revered and having her to revere was one of many affirming examples set by my family.

For that reason, my constant proximity to whiteness didn't cause me to romanticize, normalize, or idealize it. It did cause me to expiate it, however. I was always around white people and white people were always nice to me. It didn't occur to me that maybe I was palatable to white people because I was a pig-tailed, upper-middle-class little kid. I considered myself an empiricist, mainly because I was reluctant to condemn unjustly, and my experience had taught me that racism among whites was rare. If white people didn't discriminate against me as an individual, then they must not discriminate against nonwhites as a group.

I understand that there's a trope in horror movies where the protagonist will see someone she knows and begin happily interacting with him or her, only to discover that her acquaintance's body has been taken over by aliens or monsters. The protagonist feels shock, revulsion, panic, and horror. She doesn't know those she thought she did. She realizes the world isn't what she thought it was and discovers that her perspective was flawed—and that scares her. It scared me. But I didn't feel fear when a classmate told me he was moving to a public school that "was a good one without lots of minorities," or when a girl I knew described being afraid because "a big black guy" had asked her to dance at a party, I felt horror. The mask had been ripped off to reveal the ugliness underneath.

Something I also understand about horror movies is that their viewers often warn protagonists not to walk into dangerous environments. "Don't go up those stairs!" they cry. "Don't open that door!" "Are you crazy? Don't go in there!" But what do you do when your whole world is "in there"?

What do you do if the stable where you take riding lessons, the golf course where you practice your swing, the incredible museums you regularly visit are all "in there"? What do you do if your people have spent the past few centuries literally dying for your right to go "in there"? What happens when the actions and passivity of your peers "in there" reveal that the majority of them have been "body snatched"? Sometimes I'd argue with myself that my glimpses of the beings behind the masks were only tricks of the light. I had to figure out what to do with my increasing awareness that my world wasn't what it had seemed.

In my predominantly white world, addressing racism meant you were oversensitive. It meant you waited eagerly to play the "race card" and enjoyed being a victim. It meant you "made everything about race." Nonwhite people were seen as inherently biased, as unable to determine objectively what was and was not racism. I noticed that the person who criticized racism was the problem. The person who perpetrated the racism was the victim.

When I entered upper school and began to acknowledge racism, I tried to address it, always voicing my concerns and suggestions with the utmost care. I would point out to the headmaster that if I didn't love our school, I wouldn't want the student body to be more diverse; it was only because I thought the school was wonderful that I wanted more nonwhite students to attend. When I approached the upper school librarian about library books, some of them published in the past few years, that contained statements such as "abolitionists exaggerated the negative aspects of slavery," I would explain that my objection to the books' being in our collection was a manifestation of my caring for the library. I was (and remain) quiet and soft-spoken, and I rarely brought up the subject of racism. When I did, my concerns sometimes were met with the greatest respect, compassion, and, most important, positive action. I did not feel, however, as though I was always heard—such as when the principal continued to allow my teacher to wear Confederate flag ties to school.

I was coming to realize that the same people who thought I was a cute five-foot-five teenage girl clutched their purses tighter when my six-foot-one father passed them on the street. The same students and teachers who enjoyed having one or two of me in a class didn't want to be in a neighborhood full of me after dark. It occurred to me that whereas any negative action a nonwhite person took was seen as confirming stereotypes, positive actions a nonwhite person took didn't erode them. The positive actions of nonwhite individuals only allowed them to be seen as exceptions to the rule. And it hurt so badly to realize that someone I loved, someone who loved me, was racist.

I started becoming aware of the way my white environment had shaped me. Before kindergarten, when I pictured falling in love with somebody, the image was always of a guy with brown skin. Somewhere along the way, completely unconsciously, it changed to that of a white guy. As a little girl, even before I began creative writing, I would make up stories in my imagination as I waited to fall asleep. It occurred to me one day that whenever I crafted stories, all but one or two characters would be white. Again, the practice was unconscious. I wasn't choosing to dream up predominantly white characters; it was just that the environments I imagined naturally reflected the one I inhabited. Such realizations surprised, fascinated, and disturbed me. I didn't mind white people playing a part in my imagination, but it bothered me that they dominated it. Even my dreamscapes had been colonized.

My parents couldn't have been happier when I became aware of white privilege. Although almost all of our family and individual activities took place in predominantly white contexts, it was the school they had selected for my sister Ashley and me, where we spent most of our waking hours, that concerned them the most. They had picked our school because it offered a world-class education, but they wondered if the extreme lack of diversity we experienced there was too high a cost to pay. They particularly worried about me, as Ashley never struck them as assimilated. While I had always taken pride in my heritage, it wasn't until I acknowledged the presence and prevalence of racism that they were able to exhale. My radicalization meant they could relax.

On paper my parents don't seem like the kind of people who would send their children to a predominantly white school in the first place. As a little child, my black, Cherokee, English mother had adored Malcolm X the way other girls fell in love with rock stars. She admired Martin Luther King Jr., but his patience and nonviolence wearied her. In college she became fluent in Swahili, eventually teaching courses in the language. She challenged her professors on everything from the maps they used that showed Africa as disproportionately small to their neglect and distortions of African history. Her activism (and kindness and beauty) eventually won her a proposal from the king of an African country—which she politely declined.

Instead she married one of her college classmates, my father, a black Chinese man so disgusted with America's racism that he was well into his twenties before he could bring himself to say the Pledge of Allegiance. He cited prejudice in the arena of employment as a primary incentive for owning his own business. My father was baffled at how he could be given the key to the city and still get pulled over for driving while black. He occasionally entertained my little sister and me with the true story of how racist policemen once nearly arrested him for "robbing" his own parents' house.

My parents searched for schools for me when I was still a baby. In fact, my mother may have still been pregnant when they started. They visited one school where nonwhite children only a few years old spoke a variety of languages with great fluency, but, as my mother explained, "There was no joy in their eyes." At the school they ultimately settled on (when I was still under a year old), the one my sister and I would attend from kindergarten through twelfth grade, they saw a scholarly and warm faculty teaching enthusiastic students in state-of-the-art classrooms and theaters. Little kids were playing with sheep and chickens in the campus petting zoo. Older students relaxed in beautiful, colorful gardens. Everyone looked engaged, inspired, and happy. But almost everyone was white. The black and brown people around the school were cafeteria ladies and maintenance men, as well as nannies and housekeepers picking up their charges in the carpool lane. That fact concerned my parents.

So they tried to compensate, and I believe succeeded. Their efforts remind me of the "culture camps" to which white American parents send their transracially adopted children from Korea and China. During the summers, my mother taught my sister and me the nonwhite history that our school's curriculum only gave a nod to. She brewed us Cherokee pine needle tea to build up our immune systems when the moderate Houston winter began. My father taught us how gentrification was affecting the city, and our grandmother introduced us to the work of her college professor John Biggers, one of the greatest African American painters of the twentieth century.

Looking back, I find some of their tactics amusing. I remember the book of hand games my parents gave my sister and me. Most African American girls learn the clapping and rhyming games from their black friends; my sister and I had to read about them. We had books praising the beauty of skin tones described as peanut butter, warm mocha, and sweet licorice, although we were far more likely to see those shades on the people on our book pages than on those around us. Ashley could perform

West African dance. I could weave on a loom. But neither of us could claim to have black or Native American friends for the better part of our childhoods. As I said, my parents weren't really worried about Ashley's racial self-esteem. They were concerned, however, that despite my love for my cultures, I denied the prevalence of racial injustice.

I think my parents were confused. How could I be secure in my racial identity if I didn't understand the important role racism played in the world? It seems that my immediate and extended families and I debated the point endlessly when I was little. It wasn't that the discussion began with my relatives trying to convince me of the reality of white supremacy. The conversations usually started with a very real, very painful humiliation suffered by one of us the previous week, a tale retold cathartically. But what my relatives saw as prejudice, I was more likely to excuse as simple rudeness.

My sister and I would sit in our maternal grandmother, Dear's, lap, while my parents sat on either side of her wooden desk. My Creole step-grandfather would sit at the end of the sofa. My aunt Linda and my adopted African American aunt Gwen would frequently stand, animated by passion.

"Wednesday," I remember Gwen saying once, "we were asking for directions. We were in this white neighborhood, driving around looking for this restaurant, and we just could not find it. So we pulled over and asked these two white people if they knew where the restaurant was. The woman said, 'I don't, but Greg does.' And meanwhile the man was just looking around, looking at the ground. And the woman kept saying, 'Greg, you know where it is. You *know* you know where it is. Why won't you tell them?' And the man just wouldn't tell us because he didn't want us in that neighborhood."

"That's how they are sometimes," said Dear mildly.

"They do the same thing to me," added my dad. "I got a phony speeding ticket for just driving through a white neighborhood, trying to pick the girls up from school. Sometimes they just don't want us around."

"Why are your people like that?" Aunt Linda teased Grandfather.

"I'm not one of them!" he said emphatically.

"It's not fair to judge all of a race by one person," I reasoned. "Maybe Greg was just mean." What I saw as isolated incidents—though, in retrospect, continuous isolated incidents—the adults in my family saw as part of a larger pattern.

"I'm around white people all the time," I said. "My classmates and their parents and my teachers aren't like that." This was true.

But sometimes I wonder if my belief that racism was rare might have been reinforced by my environment. If white people were so bad, then why would my parents choose to be surrounded by them: in the neighborhoods where we lived, the schools they sent us to, and so on? What was I supposed to do—believe that my parents and grandparents and aunts and uncles were right in thinking that it was rare for white people to be truly free of prejudice, and still comfortably spend all my time learning and playing with them? Did they want me to live the life they designed for me without fully believing in it? Would that calm them down?

Don't get me wrong. As a little girl I sincerely believed that racism just didn't happen all that often and that bigots were as rare as hens' teeth. My belief that most people were full of sunshine and rainbows was genuine—it wasn't a coping mechanism. But I wonder what my life would have been like had I not believed those things.

I remember the arguments my dad and I would have about racism. I found it hard to believe him when he talked about the prevalence of white ignorance. But, as I said, I was an empiricist, and my dad declined to offer me proof until I was old enough not to need it. I was in my late teens before he would tell me how, after a few too many glasses of wine at parents' night, white fathers would tell him jovially, "You know, I really like black people!" Or how white mothers would flirt with him, their overtures oddly racialized. One woman told my dad, "You're so cute, like that man in *How Stella Got Her Groove Back*." Seriously. He didn't want to hurt me by challenging my view of the world, so he didn't offer any examples to bolster his assertions. And in the absence of those assertions, I simply didn't believe him. I don't always find my dad correct on racial issues, but now that I'm older, I see him as more credible—not because he has changed, but because I have.

As a little girl, when I heard my parents discussing white people, I immediately thought about the white people I knew. Did my best friend who used to put my hair in Dutch braids when I put hers in French braids think I was anti-intellectual? Did the teacher who sent me a calligraphic thank-you note for letting her exhibit my seashell collection in our homeroom secretly believe most of my peoples preferred welfare to work? As I grew up, I did indeed find that a friend's parent who had hugged and kissed me and treated me with warmth for years requested that I ask a black guy friend or cousin to the girls' choice cotillion so I wouldn't "make anyone uncomfortable," and that the friend I could talk about everything with into the wee hours of the morning believed that blacks and Hispanics had a predilection for gang violence. But looking back, I wonder if it ever occurred to my parents that if I couldn't have friendships with my class-mates at an early age uncomplicated by politics, I would have nobody else to give my friendship to. I don't believe that ignorance is blissful or even beneficial; it's just that there are no easy answers. There's no simple way to be four races in a homogenously white space.

What my family wanted, of course, was for me to use the best education available in the state of Texas to create a great future not just for myself but for my peoples. That expectation was not without precedent. Dear had used the bachelor's degree she'd earned, at a time when few women of any color went to college, to teach black, Hispanic, and white students for almost half a century in Houston's poorest public schools. She had helped integrate the Houston Independent School District and pilot one of the city's first Head Start programs. She had used her education to further her commitment to racial and social justice. Grandfather had only a fifth-grade education. When his father was crippled in an accident, he had to leave school to pick sugarcane. Still, he is an autodidact who became flu-ent in several languages. When he began his produce/Cajun foods shop, he used his Spanish skills to provide fair-paying, respectful work for im-migrant laborers. My father taught young minority men and women how to be entrepreneurs, and my mother, who during the beginning of her marriage worked as a child therapist, often cared for families with diverse backgrounds who were on welfare. My family had a history of using their knowledge and talents to benefit minority (and white) people who didn't have the same opportunities. I too loved volunteering, although my pas-sions were focused not on ameliorating racism but on endangered animals and poverty.

My mother says that when my sister and I were babies, the first time we were rained on after we had begun talking was wondrous to us. "What's this?" we had asked, tiny hands outstretched, long-lashed eyes looking upwards. The ability to use language to discuss rain heightened our ex-perience of being rained on. Similarly, my awareness of the prevalence of racism during upper school came at about the same time I began cre-ative writing. Thus my poetry, creative nonfiction, and fiction were often about institutional prejudice, white imperialist feminism, indigenous sov-ereignty, and Orientalism. As a young girl I didn't speak much in general, and spoke seldom about racism in particular. As a teen, however, I wrote profusely, frequently addressing prejudice.

Like many African and African American, Native American, and Chi-nese people, I believed that I belonged to a community made up of an-cestors, living peers, and future generations not yet conceived. As a good citizen of that community, I was responsible to all three groups. Writing for me wasn't so much about the Western end of self-expression as it was a commitment to those who had gone before and those yet to come. It was my way of speaking for those living, dead, and yet to be who could not speak for themselves. Many Chinese people believe in hungry ghosts; thus the idea that the ancestors must be fed and revered by the living. Writing allowed me to execute this responsibility. When I heard about prejudice against either my own peoples, or Amazonian Indians who were being evicted from their lands, or women in poor countries being forcibly sterilized, I sometimes felt that I couldn't get a moment's peace until I addressed the issue in my writing. It was as though my ancestors were tugging at me. I knew my aim as a writer was to be an oracle, not an entertainer.

So, strangely, it was at my predominantly white school where I forged my revolutionary ethos. Since I was a multicultural girl in a white space, I used my situation to try to bring to my peers' and teachers' attention things that they wouldn't ordinarily notice. My quest to speak truth to power was facilitated by being in one of power's centers. And I was humbled when, over time, I became a resource for my teachers on nonwhite issues.

After I graduated from upper school, I went to Dartmouth, a mainly white college in New Hampshire, the second-whitest state in the country. At my old school, melanin in an adult person's skin most likely meant he or she was a menial laborer, whereas in Hanover, the town where Dartmouth is located, melanin was a status symbol, as it automatically meant you were an Ivy League student or professor. Nonwhite people had no other roles in the town. Many nonwhite students felt uncomfortable in such a white space, even to the point of leaving the college. I was stunned by their reactions.

"I've never seen so much diversity in my life," I would say, shocked. Although Houston is an extremely diverse city, the parts of it in which I lived and moved were far whiter than Hanover and Dartmouth. With an Igbo professor and friends from Nepal and Albania, I felt as though I was on Disney's "It's a Small World" ride.

My boyfriend during freshman year was from Ghana. In contrast to the ever-present white guy of my little kid cotillion dreams, my boyfriend was a proud Asante who paired the three European tongues he was fluent in with three West African languages. We were friends whose hours spent talking, watching indie films, and listening to Ghanaian music segued into romance.

My relationship with my boyfriend seems, in ways spoken and unspoken, to have affected my relationship with my parents, especially my father. I remember, as a little girl, pointing to an ad in *Town and Country* magazine with a picture of a JFK Jr. lookalike and saying I wanted to marry a man who looked like him. My father wondered aloud why I would want to marry a guy of a race different from his. While the model's debonair smile and old-fashioned taste in clothing reminded me of my father, all my dad could see was the model's lack of melanin. But just as my parents couldn't fully believe I was secure in my heritage until I could acknowledge the reality of racism, my love for a young Asante man affirmed to them my love for my background, and perhaps my esteem for our family.

My relationship with my boyfriend was neither about race generally nor about our particular cultures specifically. We would have loved each other had we been Maori, Mayan, or Scottish. Nevertheless, much of our journey toward each other was inspired by an interest in each other's heritages. He was intrigued by my existence in the diaspora; I was enchanted by his homeland. Both before and after becoming my significant other, my boyfriend was one of my first black friends, and we looked upon each other as long-lost cousins catching up after a centuries-long separation, exploring the bounds of nature and nurture. He and I both saw our love, and our friendship, as a sort of homecoming.

Despite the fact that qualities such as integrity, compassion, and piety rather than ethnicity are what attract me to guys, my two other college boyfriends, one American and one Jamaican, were both black. Race was not a conscious factor for me in choosing to be with them, but the happy coincidence vindicated me in a "See, I haven't been maimed by my environment" way.

My friendships, like my romantic relationships, reflected the diversity in my environment. Furthermore, once I wasn't restricted to the option of having white (or occasionally Asian) friends or none at all, I could be choosier about my relationships. As a child I used to grade white people's antiracist literacy on a curve. I still have friends I love from lower, middle, and upper school who will try to excuse the Confederacy or rant about the wrongs of affirmative action, but at Dartmouth I stopped befriending people like that. The white people I made friends with at college, whether they were savvy about racial issues or were largely unaware about the extent of discrimination against nonwhites, were uniformly people I felt I could be safe with. They didn't inadvertently say racist things. They didn't deny nonwhite perceptions of reality or history.

Fortunately, despite all the diversity at Dartmouth, I wasn't as naïve as I once was. I recognized that just because Dartmouth was more diverse than what I was used to didn't mean that various racial and ethnic groups were equitably represented. The fact that elderly white women at church gave me directions to their homes and urged me not to hesitate if I needed anything didn't cause me to discount the fact that several nonwhite guys on campus described being harassed by the police.

Still, I felt comfortable at Dartmouth, not primarily because it was more diverse than what I was used to, but because, outside of my political concern with fair representation, I still didn't notice the color of the people around me. Today I care about the inequity that leads to homogenously white spaces, but for better or worse, on a daily basis I still don't notice race in my environment. Because this is such a fundamental part of my nature, I think I would have felt the same at Dartmouth even if I had been raised in primarily nonwhite spaces. By contrast, many of my peers were uncomfortable at Dartmouth. Whiteness wasn't invisible to them. These students had known something I never had: the experience of growing up in places where they were the rule rather than the exception.

So at Dartmouth I saw both how much I had and how much I had missed. As a Cherokee girl whose prep school education meant I spoke three European languages, I looked wistfully at a Diné girl whose upbringing on a reservation meant she was fluent in her people's tongue. Who was the privileged one? Who was underprivileged? Her school hadn't taught advanced math. No one in my family spoke Tsalagi. Both of us had mastered one world and sought to succeed in a second. Like many, maybe even all the nonwhite students at Dartmouth, we were seeking to be whole.

And for me, being a whole African American, Cherokee, Chinese, English woman meant that there were two things I needed to do. First, I had to seek to rectify the inequity I had witnessed in my past. Second, I wanted to take advantage of being in a diverse community for the first time in my life in order to learn more about and protect my peoples' spiritual and cultural ways of life. For me, Dartmouth represented more than the opportunity to get an extraordinary education. It was a chance to participate in communities I wasn't able to be part of previously. No more learning hand games from how-to books.

I immediately thought about these goals when I heard of Dartmouth's First Year Summer Research project. Why not use my education to address the inequity I had seen in my past by researching the experiences of poor minority workers at my privileged white school? Why not ask them what it meant to be a modern-day Atlas, not the archaic Greek mythological figure who literally bore the skies upon his shoulders, but one of the many impoverished people of color whose labors hold up a world run by the white and elite? I felt that as a creative writer, the best thing I could do to show my appreciation to the minority service workers who supported me during my time at school was to interview as many of them as possible about race and class issues, and from their interviews write creative nonfiction oral histories. Thus my project "Atlas Speaks," a portfolio of oral histories crafted from the words of minority service workers, was born. The project was based on my interest in race and space. Who was allowed where, and did they come through the front or back door? Along with race and space, I was interested in voice.

I remember one interview with a worker who had been employed at the school for decades. She told me the story of her journey from stay-at-home mom to becoming one of the school's employees, of being called by her first name by little children, of her camaraderie with her colleagues and the paucity of black teachers, and how much she valued "her babies"—the students, white and nonwhite, that she cared for. She told me of suffering from institutional disrespect and engaging in guerrilla advocacy for minority students.

"I can't tell you how much I appreciate you doing this interview," I said, as we wound down our conversation, well past the allotted hour. She looked at me and smiled.

"You are what we fought for," she said. Her tone suggested a subtext: *So you must fight for us.* The role of a storyteller in the battle for social equity was affirmed for me once more.

It was my hope that by naming the issues, planning improvements, defining realities, and articulating hopes, by acknowledging the truth of conditions at my school, I could help it become a space of diversity and appreciation. I tried to communicate to the school's employees, "This is your space. This centuries-old school, its rose-brick buildings, its tennis courts and libraries and art exhibits and outdoor bayou classroom are your spaces." They tended it lovingly, labored in it diligently, and cared for it loyally—and they had the right to be esteemed highly and compensated fairly.

But I also wanted to say to them, referring to the white paper on which I had written their stories, "This too is your space. You have a right to a place on paper, in essays. You have a right to a forum and to give testimony. You have the right not to remain silent. Anything you say just might set you or someone else free." I had reached the point in my storytelling where, instead of accepting a nearly homogenously white cast of characters, I could put the spotlight on nonwhites.

My cultural goals at college weren't like a checklist. It's not as if I said, "Well, I've done some activist ethnography, now I'm finished fighting for social justice." "Atlas Speaks" was part of my journey, not a task completed or a battle won. And it was while recognizing this fact that I began working on my second aim: joining my peoples' communities and becoming better at serving and practicing my cultures.

There were communities available on campus for students of all the cultures in my heritage. I just had to find my space. But having lots of cultures in you can be like having lots of kids: you have to find time to devote to each one. I spoke English, French, and Spanish, but should I try to learn a language from one of my nonwhite cultures? Tsalagi? A West African language such as Yoruba? Cantonese? Which one? All three? Would such a course of action make me more culturally competent, or just crazy? Should I join a group pertaining to each ethnic heritage? When I graduated, should I join alumni associations pertaining to each one too? And if I didn't, would that mean that I was prioritizing some of my cultures over others?

I ended up organizing my time more organically. I went to black student meetings and participated in Students for Africa. I helped hire the first professor of Asian American literature in the English Department and attended Asian cultural events. During sophomore summer, I lived in the African American affinity house. I wrote political articles, celebrated a range of holidays, and protested when I was called to. But there was one community I was hesitant to join.

"It's your space," said Dr. Brewer, a Dartmouth Cherokee scholar, when I discussed the matter with him in his office. "You have a good instinct for the sensitivities around issues of Native American identity," he continued. "It's your space."

"It" was the affinity house for Native Americans at Dartmouth, or NADs. I was a NAD, but a secret one. While I practiced Cherokee traditions quietly and privately, I'd entered the house only once by my junior year at Dartmouth. Since I didn't know how to dance, during the college powwows I would volunteer at the T-shirt booth, which put me metaphorically and literally on the sidelines.

"I've never gone to NAD meetings because I thought they were for people who had been raised in Native American communities. I didn't want to intrude on space that wasn't mine," I explained. And there was something else: I never referred to myself as being "part" something or the other because I knew I was not a fractured person. When my ascendants forged their cross-cultural connections, they did not break their descendants. I'm not like a plate that lies on the floor in pieces, something less than whole, diminished, disinherited. But what if in the NAD house I was seen as a broken cookie? Being multicultural is kind of like being a messy handwritten note. You have a definite message, but people will read you as they see fit; they will possibly misinterpret you or find you ambiguous. I was concerned that by being many, I would be deemed not enough. And I felt that NADs who had been raised traditionally had the right to make that judgment. I just didn't want to subject myself to it.

I said earlier that I don't notice the race of the people around me. And I guess that's true, as I spent the majority of my life in predominantly white environments. What has changed, though, is that every now and then I become keenly aware of my own heritage. I feel especially at home in the francophone African community in Paris. I feel proud walking through the streets of Chinatown. African Americans, Asians, and whites are easily accepting of my plurality on the rare occasions when it comes up. For example, no Asian has ever looked at me askance for celebrating the Chinese New Year. But because racial authenticity is such a fraught question in the Native American community, when I was considering entering the NAD community, I was particularly conscious of race(s), the community's and my own.

And then there was my appearance. I don't like to describe myself in terms of the stereotyped features attributed to each of my cultures, but I think I look African American, whatever that means. I also think I look like all of my peoples. Some people recognize Asian or Native American features in me. Others don't. Most days I'm assumed to be African American. Often I am asked, "What are you?" If you made a spectrum of people with Samis on one end and Dinkas on the other, I would have the brown color pretty much in the middle. My bust-length hair is the last auburn on the spectrum before black. My eyes are brown. People of various races mistake me for Asian Indian or being of another Southeast Asian culture.

But despite all this, Dr. Brewer was unequivocal: "It's your space." And when I attended my first NAD meeting, I was welcomed. No one questioned whether I belonged in the house on that first Thursday evening, in cooking fry bread in the kitchen on Saturdays to sell at fundraisers, or in discussions about the racism behind Dartmouth's unofficial mascot, "the Dartmouth Indian."

I joined the Native Americans at Dartmouth group the day after I spoke to Dr. Brewer, and I welcomed the sense of communion. I learned how to peyote stitch and passed on the knowledge of Cherokee medicine I had been taught by elderly relatives. I round-danced, discussed decolonizing academia, and was introduced to the wonderful world of Pendleton blankets. But it wasn't until my senior year, when I had gathered with some other Native American students in one of the dormitory basements with a Tuscarora professor, that I had an epiphany. As we talked about Europeans in America, Native Americans in the ivory tower, and what it meant to walk in two worlds, I realized that most of the Native Americans in the room had questioned what it means to be, to be accepted as, and to be located as a Native American.

"I heard the term 'blood quantum' for the first time and it confused me," said a slender Diné boy. "I went home and asked my mom, 'How much Indian am I?'" He mimicked his mother rolling her eyes and smiling. "'You're as Indian as you feel,' she told me."

"I didn't know all the stuff about Indians living in harmony with nature until I went to school," another boy added. "And I grew up on a reservation. The way we were described in books was so far from what I knew. I thought: *Is that what we did historically? Really?*"

I was surprised. Even students who were so-called full-blooded Indians, students who were fluent in Native American languages and had grown up on reservations, had been made to doubt their indigenousness and to wonder if they fit the definitions constructed by both non-Natives and fellow Indians. Other students discussed the issue of "ghost NADs," Native American students who left the NAD community either because they personally were rejected for not being "Indian enough" or because they were offended by the judgments others made.

Finally, I spoke. "That's what kept me away from the NAD community for a long time. I thought maybe I shouldn't be there since I wasn't traditionally raised. But fortunately no one ever rejected me."

"Oh, Shannon!" exclaimed a sophomore student in dismay. I had never told anyone but Dr. Brewer about my concerns in joining NAD. I think the sophomore had just thought I was especially shy. The professor looked at me in sympathy as we all affirmed to one another what Dr. Brewer had told me months ago. That we were in the right space.

Since that time, I've heard or read about the same discussions occurring among blacks, Arabs, Asian Indians, and East Asians. I recognize their concern that the culture they identify with will find them lacking, that after a lifetime of being a minority in white spaces, they might not belong in the spaces of their own peoples either.

When people ask me, "What are you?" I'm neither offended by being queried nor perplexed about how to answer. My response, like my ethnic identity, has never shifted, but just because I don't falter doesn't mean I'm not wary of being doubted or challenged. I know I'll never be the first thing that comes to mind when people picture a preparatory school student, a Greenbrier guest, or a Native American at Dartmouth, but through maturing and my experiences in college, and particularly as a NAD, I have learned that it's not just important to know who you are; you also have to affirm where you belong. That's why I joined the Native Women's Dance Society in my senior year at Dartmouth and learned to dance "fancy shawl." When powwow came that spring, I entered the circle—my space, and the space of my people—as an African American, Cherokee Native American, Chinese American, and English American. And I danced.

After graduating from Dartmouth College, Shannon was a Lombard Fellow in Mongolia and a Reynolds Scholar in Australia. She is currently a joint-degree J.D./Ph.D. student at Harvard University in African and African American Studies.

6

Thomas Lane   The Development of a *Happa*

I was born to a Japanese mother and a white father. Although my parents had taken me to Japan many times, I never felt any connection with my Japanese heritage until I went to college. After studying the Japanese language and culture during my first year at Dartmouth, I spent a summer in Japan. On that trip I fell in love with the Japanese people. Now it seems that my life can be broken into two parts, before and after college. Before college I knew I was ethnically Asian, but I refused to accept the Asian culture. Since coming to Dartmouth, however, I have learned to appreciate all aspects of being Japanese.

Dual Identity

I am a *happa*, a Hawaiian word for someone who is half Asian. I can be white, I can be Asian, or I can be somewhere in between, depending on what suits me at the time. I was raised initially as a multiethnic child. I learned Japanese from my mother and English from the world around me, and had trouble differentiating between the two languages. When I entered preschool speaking my own unique blend of English and Japanese, the teacher assumed I was mentally handicapped because she thought I was speaking gibberish. Her acceptance was critical to me at that young age, and I informed my mother that I wanted to speak only English after that point. Since that time I have considered myself a white kid with an Asian mother, abandoning my Japanese heritage for fifteen years. Ironically, my ethnic identity was shaped by a preschool teacher whose name and face I don't even recall.

I am and always have been living in two separate worlds. I was the white boy eating fermented soybeans, the Asian boy who could speak English, and the jock who played card games. As a child, I was much closer to my white father and his side of the family because of proximity and language. Most of my father's relatives live in California, so I saw my white aunts, uncles, and grandparents at every holiday and for the occasional family dinner. I saw my Japanese relatives only during the handful of times we visited Japan, but it never struck me as odd that I rarely saw them. Perhaps I would have had more respect for Japanese traditions if we had sometimes celebrated holidays in the Japanese style.

Except for Christmas, large family dinners were a dreaded event. I was the youngest cousin by eight years and never felt able to compete intellectually with my older cousins. Conversation around the dinner table was fast-paced and intellectually challenging, with quantum mechanics and the intricacies of the English language as regular topics of discussion. Most of my cousins are also half Asian, but their command of math and science made more of an impact on me than race ever did.

My best friend from the age of two was Benny Tanner, one of many *happa* friends I had during my childhood. His mother was Chinese, but everyone assumed we were brothers, even twins. Our parents used to dress us in the same clothing, and we became known as Benny-Thomas because people couldn't tell us apart. Benny's house was like heaven, with a large-screen TV, video games, and a fridge that never ran out of soda. At home I was allowed only thirty minutes of TV a week and could drink only milk or juice. Not surprisingly, I went to Benny's house as much as possible.

Benny's family was the closest thing I had to an Asian family. In fact, he was like a brother to me, and his parents were like my second parents. During the summers I practically lived at his house, feasting on dumplings and fried rice. Benny's Chinese grandmother had recently moved to America and spoke only Chinese. I learned essential phrases in Chinese, such as "wash your hands" and "who farted?" At my house, the only Asian influence was that we didn't wear shoes in the house. I did not experience the typical Asian style of parenting Benny had. He took piano lessons and went to Kumon (an afterschool math and reading program), and his parents constantly hounded him about his grades and told him to study more. My parents encouraged me to do well, but they rarely said anything about my grades while I was young.

I went to a Chinese public school for the first eight years of my education. The students were both Asian and white, yet the school was referred to as "that Asian school in San Marino." The school population was racially divided, the whites playing football and the Asians playing cards, though I did both. The few Asians who did become athletes were considered "whitewashed," and the whites who played cards were the social outcasts, as they often were fat, wore thick glasses, and ran the math club. There was racial tension at the school, but the various groups were generally formed around common interests, not the color of someone's skin or the language he spoke.

I had started doing gymnastics at around age five, and Benny did too about a year later. We joined the team in middle school and had ten or more hours of practice a week. The guys on the gymnastics team were the closest thing we had to brothers. We grew up together, went through the pain of workouts together, and played together on the weekends. They were also the biggest assholes I have ever known. They made fun of everyone on the team, and no topic was considered taboo. If you were pudgy, you were relentlessly teased for being fat. Using words like "fag," "chink," and "beaner" was considered normal. Some kids could not take the constant teasing and soon quit. These guys and our coaches turned me into an insensitive asshole, but they also forced me to stand up for what I am. I was picked on for being too short, too scared, too Asian, not Asian enough, and I had to stand up for every decision I made and fight for what I believed in. By the time I reached high school, I could handle any insult thrown at me.

In middle school I identified as white. I cracked jokes about the Chinese kids who spoke only Chinese and balked at the idea of learning Japanese. I wanted to learn something useful, like Spanish, not some language that would help me speak to my faraway grandmother. Although I never hid the fact that I was Asian, I never embraced what that meant. When asked what my ethnicity was, I would quickly respond, "I'm half Asian, half white." I spent my naïve childhood passing readily between the two worlds. I always knew that I did not fit into one group and was proud to be different.

Clashing Cultures

My parents had very different ideas about my education, and I saw little merit in my mother's views. My dad believed I would do well no matter where I was, and I subscribed to his belief that if you work hard, you will do well. My mother wanted me to get the best grades possible so I could get into the best high school possible, so I could then get into the best college possible. As long as I was doing better than a C average, my father was happy, but my mother firmly believed an A minus was a clear sign that I could have studied harder. My father led me to believe that doing well in sports and other areas was more important than academic perfection, and I felt that my mother's insistence that I seek perfection in school would cause me to do worse in sports and make me less successful overall. I felt she was wrong and viewed her suggestions as useless nagging.

This is where I thought my American upbringing clashed most fiercely with my mother's Asian childhood. Because my grades were very high, I felt I should have free rein over my education, and my mother's constant urging to study confused and angered me. I was taking the hardest classes and almost always had one of the highest grades in the class. To my mind, as long as I produced the results, it made absolutely no difference how I got there. To me, high school was a means to an end: you got good grades in high school so you could get into college. My ignorance about Japanese views on education and my mother's attempts to force me to study led to a continual battle of wills. Our conflicting views, especially about education, caused my mother and me to drift apart.

Looking back, I understand better where my mother was coming from, but at the time she seemed overbearing. I viewed social obligations and sports as my most important commitments and felt my mother was holding me back from the important things in life for something I had already conquered, my schoolwork. Ultimately, bending to my mother's rules probably had no impact on my social status, and her concerns about my studies made little difference to my academic success. I'll probably never fully understand what my mother wanted from me, but as I learn more about Japanese education, my mother's arguments and desires now carry more weight.

My parents' views on education clashed anew when it came time for me to pick a high school. My father wanted me to continue in the public school, even though it was quite some distance from home. My mother wanted me to go to a local private school, one of the best in the area. My father did not believe that the school's reputation justified the cost and doubted that it would provide a better education. My mother wanted her son to be on the best possible educational track and therefore favored private schools. The decision was ultimately left to me, and prompting from my friends led me to pick Webb, a small boarding school in southern California.

The Webb School's motto was *principes, non homines*—"leaders, not mere men." From the time I started high school, I fully believed that I was ready to become a man. The transition to high school was a huge change for me, both physically and mentally. In middle school I was small; at five feet two and eighty pounds, I was one of the shortest guys in the school. I had no idea what I wanted in life. At Webb I felt I was getting ready to become an adult and to be trained to change the world. Another important change was hitting puberty. In the summer before high school I grew several inches, gained forty pounds, put on muscle, and gained the deep voice of manhood. By the time I reached Webb, I was ready for anything.

The Webb School had about 350 students, 70 percent of whom lived at the school. It was a private school that prided itself on having a diverse student body; the students represented about a dozen countries and all ethnic minorities. Being half white and half Asian, I felt I was part of the ethnic majority. There were not any big cliques at the school, and unlike at larger public schools, being at Webb essentially forced racial integration because you knew everyone. The classes averaged fifteen students, so you were able to know all your classmates intimately, and everyone was in an advisory group composed of seven students and a faculty adviser. The advisory groups started the school year with a three-day camping trip, held weekly meetings, and did various things together such as group dinners or short trips. My freshman group was split evenly between day students and boarders and was ethnically diverse, and the boys had a wide range of skills; some had good grades, some liked sports, and some were artistic. At Webb I was exposed to true diversity, not just ethnic diversity but also diverse talents and socioeconomic backgrounds. Webb encouraged and even forced interaction with all types of students and made it hard to socialize with only a small circle of friends. Although some of the kids were definitely less popular, they interacted with the whole student community.

This is not to say racism did not exist at Webb. Although our differences were celebrated, I am sure those in the minority felt differently from those in the majority. Race was not critical, however, and a diverse group of students held leadership positions. The biggest distinction at Webb was between boarders and day students. Boarders tended to be closer because they lived together, and they resented the laxer rules and standards that day students were held to. Being a day student was the only way in which I felt I was part of a group because of circumstance rather than choice. Webb created an environment where race was essentially absent as a factor for success, and while I feel that attending Webb made me a more understanding person as a result of my interactions with many types of people, it did not enable me to experience the world for what it really was.

The sheltered world of Webb protected me from seeing the much more pronounced racism in the world around me.

Personal Preferences

My very first crush started sometime in middle school. She was a cute little blond girl named Kami. We had gone to school together since the first grade and were close friends. By the eighth grade, I dreamed of dating her but was too scared even to admit that I liked her. I met my high school sweetheart, Jen, at the beginning of my sophomore year. After being close friends for some time, we started dating more seriously. Jen was half Mexican, half white, and her parents were divorced. We dated for about three years and broke up before we left for college.

Although I did not notice it at first, my preference in girls shifted when I got to Dartmouth. I met Allison the day after moving into my dorm, and we quickly became good friends. She was Chinese, one of the first Asian girls I had found attractive. I had never noticed Asian girls before coming to Dartmouth—perhaps because the selection of Asian girls was relatively slim at my small high school. Throughout my freshman year of college, I had relationships with both white girls and Asian girls, which was a radical change from my dating preferences in high school.

The next shift began while I was in Japan, and this time I noticed. From the second I stepped into Narita Airport, I looked at the girls all around me. There was something about these ultra-skinny girls that had never struck me on my previous trips to Japan, and I felt that a completely new and unexplored world had opened to me. The ten weeks I spent studying at Kanda were amazing. Aside from my general delight at being able to live in Japan and learn the language, the three-to-one girl-guy ratio at the school was a definite plus. Because most kids at the school thought I was fully white, I received the generous attention the Japanese bestow on all foreigners.

Although my relationships in Japan were platonic, I had definitely developed an affinity for Asian girls. I spent hours watching YouTube videos of popular Asian singers and kept in contact with many of my new female Japanese friends. My taste in girls followed this Asian trend all year, but then the obsession faded, although I still find Asians appealing today. My mother is strongly against my marrying an Asian girl and has warned me that Asian in-laws tend to be more intrusive in their daughters' lives. But of course I have no idea what the future holds in terms of my relationships.

My preference in girls mirrors my cultural preferences. I was raised with Japanese foods and traditions but never really absorbed them, except to say *itadakimasu* before every meal with my parents. Once I finally started noticing all the Japanese things around me, I wanted to learn more about being Japanese. I registered for Japanese classes with the goal of going to Tokyo for further study. While studying in Japan, I continually joked with my friends that I wanted to become Japanese. Although I knew I never would be mistaken for being ethnic Japanese, I could become culturally Japanese. I especially wanted to separate myself from the *hennagaijin*, the weird foreigners who loved anime and wished they could become Japanese. I became obsessed with trying to learn about all aspects of being Japanese and with exploring the obscure parts of Tokyo. I tried to visit a different restaurant or store every day, but although I was immersed in all things Japanese, I remained just as American as ever.

After studying Japanese primary school education in a class at Dartmouth, I realized I could never become truly Japanese. My American elementary education had imprinted me with a different set of cultural values, the American ideals of individualism and capitalist success. No matter how much time I spend in Japan, part of me will always be uniquely American. Although I still want to adopt more Japanese mannerisms and speak the language well, I realize now that I do not want to be Japanese. I have been raised with American values and would have trouble with Japanese values that place the group above the individual. Moreover, although I want to understand more fully what it means to be Japanese and understand that way of thinking, I do not want to live my life according to Japanese values. When I return to Japan, my goal will no longer be to emulate the Japanese but to be invisible.

Although I was born half Japanese and half white, I have never been an equal mix of the two. As I learn more about my Japanese heritage, I feel more comfortable referring to myself as Japanese. I no longer feel like a white boy pretending to be Japanese without knowing what it means. In time I hope to close the gap between my Japanese and American sides, to feel equally comfortable with both cultures, and to be able to switch between them naturally. Although I started to learn and understand Japanese traditions during my three-month stay and was taught the importance of using the proper forms of honorifics, I still do not understand why it is so essential to use them. I may never fully understand such traditions, but I hope to be able to practice them as comfortably as I do any American tradition. I am now closer to closing the gap between my white and Japanese sides, and I look back fondly on my transformation into an American who has learned to love Japan.

I still do not fit into any single group. I am sometimes the one white boy in the Asian American Society, and at other times I am "that Asian kid" hanging out in the frat house basement. I have grown comfortable with who I am and proudly embrace the fact that I am different. Going to college changed my perspective and helped me understand what it means to be half Japanese. Although I have no definitive plans for the future, I do hope to spend at least a couple of years living in Japan, doing volunteer work or teaching English. I most likely will return to America to go to graduate school, but the future is still wide open. I look forward to seeing where my life will take me after Dartmouth.

Thomas graduated from Dartmouth after double-majoring in engineering and Asian and Middle Eastern studies. He is currently doing a rotational engineering management development program and will work in several different locations around the country before taking a full-time job.

7

Ki Mae Ponniah Heussner   A Little Plot of No-Man's-Land

The first few minutes of the bus ride were uneventful, even pleasant. I had taken a seat on the bus across the aisle from a particularly talkative classmate of mine, and found her unending stream of conversation comfortably distracting. So while Whitney and I exchanged our first-grade pleasantries, the bus made its way to school, quietly bumping up and down the length of Bedford Road. It was not until the bus rounded the corner and stopped in front of Sterling Drive to pick up two older boys that our chattering came to a standstill. Like every younger child on that bus, I too inquisitively noted the arrival of those older boys. My curiosity was replaced by apprehension, however, when I realized that they had taken the seat directly in front of mine and were peering down at me over the back of their green vinyl seat.

I was just a little girl with long black hair who had confidently boarded the school bus that morning, proud of the care she had taken in dressing herself for the first day at her new school. But all too quickly I became embarrassed, conscious that my black-and-green plaid dress looked foolishly formal next to the grubby jeans and T-shirts of the boys in front of me. And the black patent leather shoes that had been my favorites up until that moment found no friend among the rest of the sneakers on the bus. But I had not noticed any of these things until those two boys noticed me.

Under their scrutiny I felt alone. Under their wide and watchful eyes I felt dwarfed by everyone else who seemed suddenly so much bigger and tougher and better. The aisle that separated Whitney from me seemed impassable, and the back of my seat felt twice as high as it had before. I had never felt more trapped, and I had never felt more on display. And then, as though attempting to classify a bird or a snake in a pet shop, one of the boys sort of cocked his head to one side and asked, "What are you?"

"*What am I?*" I thought. I do not remember ever having been asked that question before, and if I had, it certainly had not been offered in the same way, with the same stare, and with the same suspicion. I did not know what he wanted to know. I did not understand what he hoped to find out. *What was I?* I was a girl. I was a first-grader. *WHAT am I?* Not who, but *what*, as though I had more in common with Cookie Monster than I did the human race! He must have noticed my confusion, because he continued, "You know, are you Japanese? Or Chinese? What are you?"

"Oh," I said with pride, finally recognizing what it was that he wanted to know. "I'm part Malaysian."

I was on familiar ground again, and could offer information that had elicited appreciation before. But he had never heard of Malaysia, and he started to reel off other races, as though I was wrong and had to pick one with which he was familiar. So I timidly clarified my answer for the confused boy, providing him with a response that characterized how I saw myself from that day onward.

"Well, I'm a quarter Chinese, a quarter Indian, and half, you know, American."

And it was the first time in my life that I realized that I was any different from anyone else. Before that moment I had not known that people could consider me unlike them; I was not aware that there were whole worlds to which I did not really belong. At the international school I had attended until that day, the uniforms of black, gray, white, and navy were the only colors that all the schoolchildren had in common. It was only upon leaving that school and moving to my new, predominantly white Connecticut suburb that I became conscious of race.

I have been asked that question—What are you?—countless times since that day, and by now, at twenty-one years of age, I am used to it. I do not mind the question, and I have memorized my response. To be honest, there are times when I even enjoy the frequently interesting conversation that follows. But often, when I recall the height of those green vinyl seats and the width of that impassable aisle, anger and frustration replace my usual composure. I'm no longer angry at a little boy who didn't even know that he had the power to make me feel so diminutive; he was barely older than I was, and as little as I understood about the meaning and implications of his question, I'm sure he understood far less. Any anger or frustration I feel now is directed instead toward a society that still has not learned its racial alphabet and still must search for a lexicon of acceptance. And because I quickly and quietly tucked away my personal racial questions, it is only recently that my own racial vocabulary has moved past that of the first grade.

That little boy couldn't have had any idea that his innocent question would leave such a lasting impression. I am sure he would be surprised to discover that I still remember him and the first words he ever spoke to me. But although he may never know, the awareness and the consciousness produced by our little elementary interchange quickly stole the limelight from my stage. Before I had met that boy, I was Little Orphan Annie, always harassing my parents until they allowed me to sing my favorite song for their dinner guests. I did not sing at all that first day of school, and I did not sing for a long time afterwards, either. I became a very quiet girl who caused very little trouble.

Recognizing that my differences had the potential to create discomfort for the people around me—often the people closest to me—I invariably tried to blend in as best I could in other ways. I grew far more introverted than the Lion the stars predicted I would become, and often felt more comfortable with the fictional characters in the books I read than with the real, live children in my classrooms. While children on the playground might have noted my dark hair and different features with cries of "mutt," and the adolescents in my classes found amusement in teasing me with whispers of "beast," the characters in my tales and novels never said a word. As a child, I recognized that my visible differences were the source of these names and my troubles, yet I did not know how to reflect upon the origin of these differences. I never thought to blame race; instead, I just blamed myself.

Ashamed, embarrassed, and convinced that these encounters revealed truths about my flaws and imperfections, for far too long I silently kept these stories inside. It is only recently that I have begun to disentangle these tales of the bus, the playground, and the classroom for my parents. And when I do, I sometimes hesitate, wondering if they can possibly understand the experience of a daughter who has led a life so different from their own.

My mother was born in Klang, Malaysia, to my Chinese grandmother and my Indian grandfather, and although she too grew up as a racially mixed child in a race-sensitive society, I often forget that this is an experience we share. My mother recalls that the few other children of racially mixed marriages were teased and excluded by the "purely" Chinese and Indian children, yet her memory of her own childhood is not colored by the recollection of these experiences. My grandfather was the principal of the school that my mother and her siblings attended, and their status as his children elevated their standing among their classmates. Moreover, after marrying in spite of severe opposition from their church and communities, my grandparents were fiercely protective of their mixed family, and tried very hard to instill pride in my mother, my aunt, and my uncles. As the youngest of four children, my mother recognized the support and pride of her family and easily faced the crowd of her racially "pure" classmates.

In the end, her racial and cultural impurity played a significant role in setting her apart from and ahead of the crowd. Having no other common linguistic ground between my grandmother's Cantonese and my grandfather's Tamil, and recognizing the political value of English at a time when Malaysia was still occupied by the British, my grandparents insisted that their children speak only English at home. At that time, many Malaysians could speak English but few could claim it as their first language. My mother's unusual proficiency in English played an integral role in distinguishing her from her university classmates in Malaysia.

While my mother was singing hymns at a college that was left as a gift to a developing country by British missionaries, my father was still tossing footballs across a high school stadium in Bay Village, Ohio. While my mother was awaiting her marriage to the first man she had really known beyond a few conversations, my father was preparing to escort his date to the senior prom. And while my mother was preparing for a life that would not take her very far from home, my father was hoping to take his intellect and athletic ability from his small midwestern town to the Ivy League.

About five years later, in Boston, only a couple of years after my father had graduated from college and my mother had left her first marriage, their different worlds overlapped at a joint lecture between their two graduate schools. As the story goes, they met one afternoon, went for a cup of coffee, and married soon after at the university chapel. Seven years later they had me, and one and a half years after I was born, they divorced.

There have been times when, perhaps out of anger, I have wondered what my parents could possibly have been thinking, to believe that two people from such different backgrounds, histories, cultures, and countries could actually remain happily married forever. There have been other times when, perhaps out of puzzlement, I have wondered if my parents were merely intrigued by the exoticness of the other. And, finally, there have been times when, perhaps out of loneliness, I have wondered if they ever thought about what it might mean for their child to grow up in a no-man's-land between their two cultures.

At my worst, I have questioned their motivation in deciding to have me at a time when their marriage must already have begun to unravel. How dare they bring a child into the world when they were still struggling to find within it a place for themselves together? And what kind of parents could they possibly be if they failed to imagine what it would be like for their own child to grow up—inherently like them both and yet nothing like either of them?

Perhaps it is not my place to determine if my parents' marriage broke down primarily along the fault lines of culture or love. But in seeing that the worlds my parents have entered and cultivated since their divorce exaggerate the differences that existed before they married, I think I will always blame culture, at least in part. I know that whatever tale I tell will not be able to capture completely my relationships with them and their respective worlds. And I know that even the boundaries of these worlds I imagine are not as strict and defined as I often think they are. But still, regardless of the overlap that exists, these worlds are much more antagonistic than they are compatible, as the word *divorce* suggests.

My parents' split took them swiftly to their new, separate lives. And in the process, it ruptured the integrity of my multicultural world and set in motion a lifelong seesaw ride between their two cultures. I am learning to put my parents' past behind me, yet I cannot pretend that the past does not frequently take hold of the present. When I feel inextricably caught between their two worlds—rejected by both, or too quickly accepted by one—I wish to be solely of one heritage. I do not think people often realize how much of a luxury it can be to have one group to fall back on, one to blame, or one to identify with and one to reject. Perhaps it's easier to wear your racial consciousness on your sleeve when you know that you can always hide behind the garb of an entire race if things get too bad, or if the opposition comes on a little bit too strong for you alone. Most will never know how much more difficult it is to speak out when you feel as though you have to pick a side, even though *neither* side is really your own.

For as long as I can remember, I have searched my parents' faces and their collections of old photographs, hoping to find some connection between who they have been, who they are now, who I am, and who I will be. Most children cringe when neighbors and relatives tug them closer and exclaim at the resemblance between parent and child; I stood a bit taller on the few occasions when people saw my parents in me. Even when I was in the prime of my adolescence, the peak of my rebellion, I remained the well-behaved daughter who desperately wanted to please *all* her parents—biological and stepparents alike. When I should have been attempting to create an identity and an ideology of my own, I still held back.

If my bus ride to the first day of school marks the first time I recognized my differences in relation to the people around me, an evening with my father a year or two later marks the first time I really recognized the significance of my differences in relation to my own family. And although the initial recognition came over a decade ago, it is primarily over the past few years that I have learned how much more painful and difficult it is to negotiate differences within a family than with the people outside it.

After a busy day spent touring another one of New York's many cultural gems, my father, Bonnie (then his fiancée), and I found respite on the living room floor of my father's West Side apartment. It was almost time for me to go to bed, but after flipping through the television channels, we decided to watch the end of the Miss America pageant. During one of the commercial breaks, in a good-natured attempt to compliment Bonnie, my father commented, "What do I need to watch this for? I have the most beautiful woman in the world right here."

Instead of merely accepting his flattery with appreciation, being sensitive and female herself, Bonnie looked over at me and quickly interjected, "Dale, don't you mean the *two* most beautiful women in the world?"

At first my father looked completely confused and did not understand the reason for her prompt. It was only when he followed her glance over to my face that he recognized my disappointment and revised his previous remark.

I will admit now, with a tinge of shame, how much it mattered to me that my father revised his original comment, but at the time I was too embarrassed to say a word. Perhaps it is not important for a parent to think his child beautiful, but when I was seven years old and just recognizing that I looked different from most people around me, my father's casual comment struck a chord I did not know existed until that moment. I was not a vain child in need of praise, but I did not want to be excluded from my father's definition of beauty. I did not want to feel any more self-conscious or be reminded yet again that I did not look like my father's daughter.

Now I accept our lack of resemblance and no longer agonize over the reaction our differences inevitably provoke. When I was a teenager too tall for her age, however, I used to fear that, without Bonnie along, people would mistake me for my father's girlfriend. And when my father, Bonnie, my brother Jesse, and I would wander about Westport, Connecticut,

I would worry that people might assume that I was Jesse's nanny and not his sister. In a town where most Asian women are nannies, who would expect that the one Asian female walking with a little blond-haired, blue-eyed boy and his equally Caucasian-looking parents could be related to them by blood?

Over time I have grown comfortable with the place I occupy within and between my two families, and I have come to value the unusual pictures we paint together and apart. But it is only recently that I have been able to appreciate and navigate this space that often feels very lonely. In the twenty-one years of my life, my father and I have spoken only a few times about our cultural differences. And although we frequently laugh about the unexpected family portrait we must present to onlookers in restaurants and shops, I sometimes think he underestimates the extent of those differences. Both he and Bonnie have always encouraged me to speak my mind, but I really do not know how I would begin to enumerate to them the differences between life at his house and life at my mother's house.

When they ask for my "honest" thoughts on how they raise Jesse, how do I tell them that, because I was raised in my mother's house, where "tough love" reigned and gifts were never used to appease temporarily, I have often wished that they were not so generous with both me and Jesse? And when I open up the trash can and see piles of still edible food and still usable plastic utensils, how do I honestly reveal that, because my stereotypically penny-wise Chinese grandmother would cringe at the amount of things wasted in their home, I tend to cringe inwardly as well? Moreover, how do I honestly express the guilt and dismay I often feel when I recognize that many of the characteristics I criticize in my father's world have managed to find a place in me? I have no blueprint to follow, I have no paradigm to respect, and I cannot always tell if honesty is healthy or hurtful.

At my mother's house, I am not alone in negotiating multiple worlds; my mother and stepfather's marriage also crosses racial and cultural lines. But because my stepfather has spent almost as much time in Asia as my mother has in America, they have been able to help my sister Maylien and me to navigate the blurred cultural cross-sections that characterize our lives. Yet even so, there are times when I have to stop myself from too easily following my mother's and stepfather's bad habit of prematurely dismissing those who have not trodden the same ideological path they have. Both professionally and personally, their lives have taken them to more countries than most people in our town are probably able to identify, and as a result they recognize the degree of global inequity far more

deeply than even our most well-traveled neighbors. Their model of justice is based on a global understanding of the injustices that they have
perceived in the world, and they have passed this understanding on to my
sister and me. The most difficult lesson for us all to learn is to appreciate
our own experiences without detaching ourselves from those whose lives
do not cross so many cultural boundaries.

Here in America, the various cultures that have found a home under
one roof have, over time, integrated harmoniously to form a new whole.
The cultural differences, however, between my mother's family and the
new family we have created emerge profoundly when we make our bien-
nial trips to Malaysia and find ourselves held to the standards of a society
we're only a small part of, and that is only a small part of us.

Although my friends are fond of reminding me that I inflect the tone
of my voice far more than I should, the inflection and cadence of my own
voice is *nothing* compared to the ruckus of my Malaysian family's conversation. When the whole *jinbang* is assembled, conversation is dotted with
"ah!" and *"Ai yo!"* and phrases are punctuated with the local *"lah."* What
might be lacking in vocabulary is compensated for with animation. Lively
hand gestures substitute for unnecessary words, and volume often trumps
text. If we are lucky, Uncle Vinci will surrender and buy the delicious,
grease-saturated *roti chenai* and chicken curry. If we are patient, we will
catch the nightly stroll of the *chee-chak* (lizards) who emerge from their
daytime hiding spots. Yet if my sister and I are loud, we, being female, will
provoke the criticism of our older uncles, who will quickly remind us that
we have become "too American."

When Maylien and I linger around the dining room too long after eating dinner, our uncles artfully push us along to the kitchen sink; when
we are caught reaching for another biscuit at teatime, we are asked, with
a pat on the belly, if we *really* want another. *"Ai yo*, you girls," Uncle will
say, clucking his tongue loudly, "you spend too much time in that country." Although he teases with a good-natured smile and mocks us with a
disarming grin, there is firm conviction behind his words. He jokingly
refers to his American nieces as lost causes, but I think he does believe
that there are standards set for Asian women, and he certainly believes
we should respect them. If Uncle Vinci had his way, all of the women in
his life—sisters, daughters, and nieces alike—would match the image of
his slim young wife. Auntie Swee Gin has the smooth, long hair, the slim
build, the pale skin, and the coy demeanor of the ideal Asian woman. And
although the rest of us poke fun at the adoring glances and reverent words
she bestows upon my uncle, there have been times, especially when I was

younger, when I wished I could escape the tyranny of my uncle's criticisms by more closely resembling her.

In America, by contrast, the coyness and reserve of the demure Asian female are met with mixed reviews. Although I may have been too loud for my Asian uncles in Malaysia, I think I have often been too quiet for my American family and friends at home. And if I attribute the silence of my childhood to the simple recognition of race, I believe that my adolescent reticence is due to the echoes of my uncles' warnings. I certainly did not back down from conflict and confrontation to please those uncles, but I think that I found in their model—or at least in the one they projected— the best balance to the imposing height and academic success that I sometimes wanted to hide.

I thought that if I could not change the appearance of "beast," perhaps I could distract people with the demeanor of "beauty." To a thirteen-year-old girl whose big red glasses covered the upper half of her face, whose height seemed to give away her presence in a crowd of two hundred, and whose dark hair and slightly off-kilter features refused to cooperate to create something pleasing or familiar to look at, any distraction that might minimize the awkwardness was eagerly accepted.

Those painfully awkward years did not last as long as I dreaded they would. I amended the mistake of the large red glasses by trading them in for a pair of contact lenses. And soon after, I somehow sufficiently grew into the features and height that had plagued my early adolescence. I was no longer the quietest girl in my class and, as I grew, so did my confidence and the strength of my voice. Yet I was far from outspoken. Even after I did not need the "ideal" demeanor to offset a less-than-ideal appearance, I still held on to the quietness and reserve that had characterized my earlier behavior.

Throughout high school I was considered a leader of my class, and I appreciated the distinction and respected the responsibility. But even though I could muster up the courage to address administrators and speak professionally with teachers, I found it difficult to interact with many of my peers with the same amount of confidence. A child of a practically TV-less home, I took a while to recognize pop culture. And as a child of a multicultural, international home, I could more easily identify the name of a UN agency than a Fortune 500 company. As a result, I would often find myself mid-conversation with little to say, searching frantically for common ground. Wanting neither to accentuate my differences by pleading cultural ignorance nor to check out of the conversation completely, I would linger at the edges, smiling and nodding appropriately, wondering when the trial would end. I was a good student and the president of my class, but when I interacted with many of my classmates, I found myself constantly questioning the cadence of my speech and the formality of my language. I created multiple voices to fit the multiple worlds I encountered in my life, and when I could not tailor the appropriate voice to a given situation, I chose silence.

For a long time, I think I believed that the integration of these worlds would come once I met someone who would let me be myself all the time. But when I was younger, I would become so enamored with someone that in his presence I would lose the capacity to speak. Although I might write pages and pages about how wonderful, unique, and perfect "he" might be, in the face of opportunity with him I would become so nervous that I would find myself unable to form thoughts and compose questions. And when our conversation eventually reached a standstill, I would be left wondering if the person I had created with my pen really did exist beyond the pages of my journal. As I grew older, confidence lent me the ability to carry on a conversation, but I still would never learn the true nature of my pen's inspiration. As the rules dictated in this odd game I would play, the second I sensed reciprocated interest, I would completely lose interest, until, of course, I felt that interest had been lost in me.

In middle school and high school I easily excused this pattern by declaring the high standards I held for myself. It was not that *I* was the one who lacked the capability to get to know someone beyond a first date or a first kiss; it was more that I honestly believed that my exceptional powers of perception enabled me to sense incompatibility from a mile away. I know now that I was deceiving myself. It was not always high standards or perception that prevented me from getting too close to anyone romantically, or even platonically for that matter. I was just too insecure, and I lacked the confidence to believe that anyone could really like me; if he did, then surely something about him must be wrong.

A few months after coming to college, however, I did meet someone who seemed absolutely flawless to my freshman eyes. And although now I sometimes wonder how Jon and I managed to maintain any type of relationship at all over the years, I think, at least to a degree, that what kept us together was equally responsible for ultimately pulling us apart. While my family life has been unique, his has been quite conventional. My views are liberal, his are conservative. And my background is mixed, his is not. Now that our three-year on-again, off- again relationship has finally reached its conclusion, I look back amazed at how long we attempted to make our relationship work. Sometimes I think that had we just been disciplined enough to stop ourselves from falling back to each other, we might have developed other, more complementary relationships. But I also know that for a very long time, I refused to let go of the security and comfort my first serious romantic relationship offered, despite the many clues and conversations that indicated that our relationship would inevitably someday end.

The first time Jon forced us to confront our increasingly apparent differences, I thought it was the last time we would ever speak. We had certainly been aware of these differences from the beginning, but we enjoyed the sometimes amusing, sometimes exasperating conversations they created. Only four months after we started dating, however, those same qualities that had initially amused and intrigued us began to divide us. During the summer after my freshman year in college, when I was at home and Jon was at school, and our relationship existed over telephone lines and extended weekends, our incompatible qualities became irreconcilable differences. Toward the end of the summer, when I anxiously noted the infrequency of his calls and sensed the detachment in his voice, I asked him what was wrong. And he simply replied, "We're just so different."

Refusing to continue over the telephone, I drove up to school the following weekend to finish our conversation in person. Between a Saturday afternoon and a Sunday evening, we uncovered every foreseeable difference that could possibly limit our capacity to sustain a relationship. Toward the end of the weekend, when our religious, philosophical, personal, and political debate was already threatening to turn my boyfriend back into a stranger, he asked the question that I may silently remember each time I begin a new relationship. "Well," he offered timidly, "what if I don't know how I'd feel if my children didn't look like me?"

At the time, his question did not unsettle me any more than the rest of the conversation had. Instead of listening to what his question revealed, I simply dismissed it with a frown and stumbled my way through a response: "I just don't think you need to know that right now.... Shouldn't we just be thinking about *now?* I guess I just don't understand why we need to talk so much about the future...."

I should have appreciated his honesty, and I should have followed his inquisitive lead, but I was not prepared to consider the possibilities of such a far-off future, and I was too scared to acknowledge the questions that could threaten that and future relationships. I thought I already knew the familiar, discouraging answer, and I forced myself to ignore it.

Aside from my family, no one else in my life challenged me to confront race in such a personal way, and at times I was disappointed in the shortcomings, within each of us, that were revealed in the process. Yet

three years of disagreement and reconciliation allowed us both to examine mindfully, and sometimes adjust, what we had always believed to
be true.

During my adolescent years, when my journal reflected the innocent
musings of a naïve teenage girl, I thought that upon falling in love I would
be transformed into someone more confident, self-assured, and independent. I had hoped that one person would be able to help me integrate
the different worlds I had tried so hard to keep apart. It was not until after
dividing my worlds even further that I finally learned how to bring them
together.

Whereas in high school I was a school leader and swore that I would
someday "change the world," I spent my first years in college more concerned with social image than social awareness. Instead of setting off on
my planned path of righteousness, I sharply delineated the social aspects
of my life from the ideological ones. I took advantage of the few academic
opportunities I had to incorporate my beliefs into my academic studies by
writing about the gender-relations and social issues that I did not tackle
in my daily life. I would write papers for my English classes comparing
the roles of women in various plays, or taking a feminist stance against
metaphors in early American literature. I was even a member of an a cappella group devoted to spreading messages of social awareness through
song. Yet I did little more from day to day than sing about issues or write
about them or speak about them when the occasion arose; I did not do
nearly as much as I could have actually to *solve* the problems I claimed to
feel so strongly about. I would write about social injustice and I would
sing about female empowerment, yet at the same time I became part of
an organization—a sorority—that actively excluded women and a system
that passively divided them.

Although I decided to attend the college I did almost in spite of its
well-known Greek system, when the time came I still signed my name to
the list of sophomores looking for a bid to join one of the campus's many
sororities. I was the last woman in my class to sign up for rush and perhaps one of the least enthusiastic, because I believed that I already had the
most supportive "sorority" in my a cappella group. But even though it was
mostly curiosity that led me to the system, it was vanity that enticed me
to join. I was flattered by the offers of acceptance, and I was tempted by
the trappings of belonging. I cannot go back in time and erase my name
from the long list of sophomore rushees, but had I known then what I
do now, I would never have threatened bonds of true friendship with the
often superficial ones of "sisterhood." Now, while I am grateful for some

of the friendships formed within my sorority, I think I will always see my participation in the Greek system as more of an educational detour than a step forward in life.

It was not until fall term of my junior year that the multiple worlds in my life began to grow together and the words I sang with my a cappella group began to resonate in my classes and in the friendships that I formed. I finally felt engaged and productive in classes that provided me with the tools I could use to do something more someday than simply sing freedom songs to distracted college students. In the Education Department I met professors and students who powerfully influenced my life—socially, academically, and ideologically.

In a class discussion that term, our teaching assistant asked us to write down how our life would be different if we were a member of a different race. As my classmates furiously wrote their answers down, I just sat quietly and refused to write a word. People read their answers out loud and every answer began with "If I were [insert racial difference here], I would [insert racial stereotype here]," as though with a flip of a switch you would call yourself by another name, changing only the attributes associated with that name. If I were a different race—if I were only *one* race— my entire life would be different, and to think that I could be expected to enumerate, isolate, and analyze how almost offended me. To me, the question implied that you are your race, you are only your race, and your racial identification is the one that is the most important. Of course I think that people should participate in interracial discussions, but constantly defining people and groups along racial lines seems to me to be the kind of racial division that interracial discussions should attempt to move beyond.

In interracial discussions like the one my class had that day, I had always felt obliged to pick a side, as though if I did not, I would be a coward straddling a racial fence. In our racially polarized world, it often feels as though someone long ago decided that in order to have your voice count and mean something, you need to identify with one party or the other. If, of course, you attempt for some reason to identify with both and take the time to look for the middle ground, you are selling someone short, or you are not realizing all that there is in yourself, or you are taking the easy way out.

It was not until I went to China on a foreign study program the summer before my senior year in college that I fully recognized that there is no easy way out; the world's racial spectrum is far more complex than the black-and-white one many Americans think exists. I cringe at the implication that my trip to China was a quest for "roots," but in truth, I did go to China in search of a connection to the stories and traditions that peppered my childhood. My Chinese heritage is only a part of my cultural whole, but my grandmother's superstitions are still a fixed part of my daily internal dialogue. When my right eye shakes, I wonder what kind of good fortune will come my way, and when the palm of my left hand itches, I wonder how much money will soon be slipping out of it. When I forget to clean my plate, I remember my grandmother's warnings that I will then marry a pockmarked husband, and when I wear red, I immediately feel protected by the power of its lucky hue.

Before I arrived in China, and during my first days there, I hastily assumed that these superstitions, and the other relics of Chinese culture inherited from my grandmother, were enough to secure for me a comfortable connection to the Chinese people I would meet. I thought that because many of the traditions I would find in China were the ones I was accustomed to at home, I would not experience the culture shock anticipated by many of my white classmates. My motivation for traveling to China was certainly more personal than it was academic, and I expected that it would be something akin to a homecoming—if not for me, then at least for my grandmother, vicariously, through me. But I soon and sadly learned that although my family's version of "Chinese" and the "Chinese" whom I encountered in China share many qualities, my family and I are quite alone in our cultural habits and beliefs. Although many of the words we speak, the expressions we borrow, and the foods we eat are gifts from my grandmother's Chinese heritage, too many other cultures have added their own flair for us to recognize the truly "Chinese" in our lives.

As I walked and biked the streets of Beijing that summer, as I sat on buses and trains up and down the coast and back and forth across the country, and as I talked to and laughed with people and suffered their laughter at me, I found myself struggling to determine how I belonged to China and how it belonged to me. Visually, I blended into crowds of Chinese people better than I could ever hope to blend into crowds of Caucasian Americans. If you casually glanced my way and didn't experience the amusement of listening to my broken, incorrectly inflected Chinese, you might think that I had lived in China all my life. But because of my linguistic shortcomings and a mismatch between what I expected to feel and what I actually found, instead of experiencing the homecoming I had expected, I felt locked out of the culture I had hoped to be welcomed into.

One night, on a train bound for a coastal town sixteen hours northeast of Beijing, when my classmates had managed to achieve uncomfortable sleep and I was left to my thoughts, I realized that the best I could ever hope for was partial cultural understanding from any person I would ever meet outside my family. And I realized that even within my family—because of interracial marriage, divorce, and remarriage among my parents, my stepparents, my aunts and uncles, and even my grandparents—individuals are sometimes left quite alone to their cultural understandings and beliefs. On my mother's side of the family, it would be difficult to find two people other than my mother and her siblings who have an exact racial match. And although we have all benefited greatly from the synthesis of all these races, I wonder what we have sacrificed and surrendered to become a family that has had to dilute each culture in an attempt to integrate them all. And although I often relish my lack of cultural commitment, there are many moments when I would like to be able to claim one culture, commit to one culture, and be comforted by one culture only.

The more of a mix any person becomes—of experiences, of ethnicities, of cultures that are racial or not—the more she becomes connected to other people, the more she is able to understand, and the more she is offered to share. But somewhere down the line in the sharing of cultures, you realize that when each culture is done sharing for a little while and goes back to its own world, you are still left in the middle of them, dependent on them all—but alone, without any.

Most people receive their inheritance the day their parents die. I received mine the day I was born. And although I have spent much of my life running away from the little plot of no-man's-land my parents left for me to till, I am learning to enjoy the responsibility of cultivating this familiar, untapped place. The boundaries are not as rigid as I once thought they were, and the ground is much more fruitful than I originally assumed it to be. Sometimes its solitude halts my progress for a while, and sometimes I stop for a rest someplace else, but I return to my quiet lot with pride, for my entire family, for myself, and for the vision of what it might someday be.

After graduating from Dartmouth, Ki Mae worked for a U.S. senator, a microloan fund, and then Lifetime Television before returning to school for a master's degree in journalism. She currently lives with her husband in New York, where she writes about technology.

8

Samiir Bolsten   Finding Blackness

"When black people marry outside of the race, it waters us down, it is destroying our race," my friend's mother claimed while stopped at a red light. Her head slightly turned so that my girlfriend and I could hear her in the backseat. My friend's mother, a black woman in her late thirties, was driving my black girlfriend and me home. Accelerating again as the light turned green, she continued, "That's why it feels so good to see a young black couple. We start marrying their men and they start taking ours. It's ruining our race." At this point I had to make this woman aware that I was not comfortable with her sentiments, considering the fact that my mother is white.

"Actually, ma'am, I am the product of an interracial relationship and marriage," I started to say, as the car was coming to a halt in the parking space outside the train station. "I'm half white." I saw the disbelief on her face as she turned to look at me.

"No," the woman said, clearly startled. She looked me up and down as if to understand how she could have overlooked something that should be so obvious. Her problem was that my white heritage is hard to spot at first glance, as I have a relatively dark complexion for a mulatto. At a loss for words, she continued to study me before stumbling over three or four apologies. As I sat in the back of the car listening to her incomplete sentences and halting attempts to backpedal, I could only reflect on the fact that I was in familiar territory.

I was used to dealing with awkward and offensive situations related to race, having grown up with my dark complexion in predominantly white Denmark. Later on, as my family moved to more diverse environments, perceptions of me changed—both in my own eyes and in the eyes of others. It seemed that because of my unusual family situation and racial makeup, I was always perceived as different from the norm, no matter where we relocated. Although this led to issues of low self-worth and some turbulent times mentally, I eventually became comfortable with always being different. Much of this comfort came from realizing that norms were by no means rules, and that all people had some way in which they were different.

A stereotype or norm can never define a person completely, and every identity has a story behind it. Regardless of how much one adheres to social norms, the emotions and struggles we carry inside create a unique human. I eventually saw my struggle to fit the norm as a chance to understand the world better, as well as myself. My unique background forced me to realize that norms did not apply to me, and I eventually used this realization to gain a deeper understanding of myself beyond the pressures of stereotypes. This required me to begin viewing myself and others outside of the racial scope in order to get a deeper appreciation for individual identities. Because discounting race contradicted how it first shaped my identity in every way, the road to self-understanding was long and arduous.

My mother was born and raised in a middle-class family in Ballerup, Denmark, a town of about forty thousand with a very small colored population. Because of her strict upbringing, she focused on working and moved out on her own as early as she could. High school was my mother's highest level of education. During her late teens, she went on vacation with her mother and sister to Morocco. My father, who is only one year older than my mother, was selling souvenirs to tourists in Casablanca. He spent his days standing on a street corner, selling cheap ceramics and pickpocketing tourists who appeared rich. From what I understand, this is where he met my mother.

Given the bits and pieces of the story that I have picked up from my mother and father throughout the years, it appears that their interactions were nothing more than a teenage love affair. To this day I am unsure how they communicated, because my father's English is very poor and I know my mother never spoke Arabic. Regardless of how they communicated, my father gave my mother a souvenir she was not expecting: my older sister, Farrah. I am not sure exactly what happened over the next few months, but I know that my father moved to Denmark and eventually wed my mother. The circumstances under which my parents met did not exactly provide a stable foundation for a relationship or marriage.

My father had a rough upbringing in Morocco as the youngest of seven children. Being the youngest left him essentially forgotten by his parents, and he seldom had his needs met. At times he did not even own a pair of shoes. My father was rather uneducated, which may have contributed to the poor quality of his life. By the time he was twenty, he had completed the Danish equivalent of middle school with a passing grade in all his subjects.

When my father immigrated to Denmark in his late teens, he had problems finding work and turned to a life of crime and drugs. During a psychotic episode brought on by drugs, my father caused a ruckus in a nightclub by wielding a large kitchen knife. I never fully understood how this story ended, aside from the fact that he was apprehended, deemed mentally unstable, and sent to a mental health institution rather than a regular prison. Because of this, for a period in my childhood I barely saw my father, who was virtually the only black male influence in my life at the time.

I was born on February 10, 1986, in Ballerup. It ultimately turned out that my mother and father were not meant for each other, and they divorced less than a year after I was born. My father still lived in the same town, but he did not provide much support for my mother, who was now alone and raising two black children in a predominantly white town. She once told me that people would approach her to compliment her beautiful children, assuming she had done a good deed and adopted them from a Third World country. My mother has vividly described on several occasions how these people's facial expressions changed from admiration to disgust once they found out she had given birth to these two dark children. As my mother described it, their view of her instantly changed from a noble humanitarian to "someone who fucked a nigger." Before I was even able to comprehend the issue of race, my mother had suffered on my behalf, being judged and labeled by others.

Although I was a Danish citizen born in Denmark, and spoke only Danish, my skin color caused people to classify me as an immigrant, or at the very least to associate me with the resentment they had toward immigrants. When looking at me, they instantly felt they were looking at a product of parents from some war-ridden nation who came to Denmark to leech off the state. When they saw me, they assumed that my ignorant immigrant parents were raising me according to their ignorant immigrant culture, which would certainly be detrimental to what Denmark stood for. The xenophobic nature of many Danes reminded me constantly of my skin color, and therefore my inherently subordinate status.

During most of my childhood we were lower middle class, living in an apartment with my mother's boyfriend Jakob (who was white), my mother, my sister, and my half sister (who is also white). Growing up, I seldom had someone to teach me the things that most people learn from their parents, particularly boys: how to treat women, how to drive, and so on. Jakob played the biggest role in raising me, for which I am incredibly thankful. Yet even Jakob's unconditional love could not teach me what it meant to be a black man, particularly in a town like Ballerup and a country like Denmark. I was completely on my own in trying to figure out what my complexion would mean for my life.

Although we always had food, my mother and Jakob struggled financially, perpetually living paycheck to paycheck below the poverty line while trying to raise three children. My family's financial hardships, coupled with the fact that my skin color was so different from the other children's, made me uncomfortable and self-conscious in school. Most of my friends had parents who were married, educated, had stable jobs, and were significantly older than mine. My school luckily provided free lunch, which hid my family's status on the lower end of the socioeconomic spectrum. Unfortunately, the cafeteria workers went on strike when I was in second grade, and all the students were required to bring their own lunch to school for the year. My lunches, consisting of butter and cheese sandwiches on white bread and orange juice poured into a jar, were rather embarrassing next to my peers' purchased meals of chicken subs and hamburgers, which their parents dropped off for them.

I also dreaded field days, as they were typically ski trips. While my friends were downhill skiing with their brand-new ski equipment or snowboards, I had to cross-country ski using Jakob's old equipment from the 1970s. Sometimes my family situation even affected my schoolwork, such as when we were supposed to do a report on our parents' profession, I had nothing to report on. Even when I began playing soccer, getting dropped off on the back of a bike rather than being driven to practice in a car highlighted the difference between my peers and me. And then, of course, the constant exclamation point: I was "The Black Kid."

As my biological father turned to a life of crime and drugs, his relationship with my sister and me deteriorated steadily. During the early years of my life, my sister Farrah and I would spend a night at his apartment every two weeks. We used to play soccer, cook, watch movies, and sit around while he smoked cigarettes and spoke in Arabic with his friends. At this point I was still too young to realize all the ways in which my father was not fulfilling his paternal duties to my sister and me, and to my mother. The most significant thing I remember him teaching me was how to deliver a headbutt properly—snatching a man forward by his collar and meeting his momentum with a forehead crashing into the bridge of his nose. My father's role as my sole (yet almost nonexistent) black male influence caused me to associate such behavior with what I perceived to be black masculinity.

My relationship with my father and other colored people gave me no model for what my identity and demeanor should be as a black person. All I knew was that my identity could not possibly be like that of my peers because there was always something reminding me that I was different and inferior. I faced ridicule in school and on my soccer team, and fought often. Hearing "Nigger!" shouted at me was no rarity, and it came from children both my age and older. Sometimes it made me sad, sometimes angry. Regardless of my external reaction, internally the word affected me the same every time, as it was part of a system of checks and balances that ensured "niggers" would be kept in their place at the bottom of the totem pole. I had no way to find anything positive about being black, nor anyone or anything to identify with. Instead, I spent the first eight or nine years of my life loathing my skin color and the things that came with it. I remember being in music class in the second grade and looking at my friend's hair, wishing mine were straight like his; dreading soccer practice because my shorts exposed the dry skin on my legs. The other kids did not have to worry about ashy legs because it wasn't visible on their white skin. Ashy skin is of course normally visible on black children, which is why black parents know to moisturize it properly. Unfortunately, because I was the only black child and my mother was white, it only highlighted the differences between my peers and me.

Feeling like an outcast, I spent a great deal of time by myself. I enjoyed activities that allowed me to express my creative side: sports, music, and art. During very early childhood, I often occupied myself by building (not playing) with Legos, drawing, and engaging in just about any form of art that allowed me to express myself. Because I typically excelled at these activities, I felt the most comfortable while involved in them, and in school they gained me social acceptance. Ultimately, however, I was still uncomfortable being black because I found no advantage in being outside the norm.

Then *The Fresh Prince* came.

In 1990 Will Smith was offered the chance to star in his own television sitcom, titled *The Fresh Prince of Bel-Air.* The show became a huge success in the United States and went on to be broadcast in several nations across the world, one of them being Denmark. Will "Fresh Prince" Smith became one of the first positive images of a black male I had, and I instantly felt like I should and could relate to his character. I changed my behavior and acted more like the character I saw on the television screen; I could identify with him. Smith's character grew up in inner-city Philadelphia and was uprooted to live with his rich uncle in Bel-Air. Seeing him adapt to his new environment by taking advantage of his status as an outsider intrigued me and inspired me to wonder if I could do the same. Essentially, Smith was creating something positive out of being the one who always stuck out. I concluded that the natural way for me to do the same was to act like he did. I found comfort in being a class clown, using my outsider status as a way to control people's attention rather than to catch their attention unwillingly with my dark complexion or curly hair.

Once I realized that the Fresh Prince was not just a cool person on TV but also a rapper, I instantly took an interest in his music and its genre: rap/hip-hop. I thought rapping was cool mainly because the Fresh Prince did it, and I idolized him mainly because of the show. Rap music remained a loose interest of mine, as it was hard to access in Denmark. So I had to be satisfied with watching shows like *The Fresh Prince of Bel-Air.* I watched *The Fresh Prince* and other American shows so much that I learned to speak English fluently, and I began gaining a deeper interest in music as I started to understand more of the lyrics.

Then 2Pac came.

In February 1996 a Los Angeles–based rapper, 2Pac (also known as Tupac Shakur), released rap music's first-ever double disc, titled *All Eyez on Me.* Because of the album's incredible success, 2Pac's fame extended far beyond U.S. borders and made its way to my television and radio in Denmark. Tupac Shakur was another of my first major influences as a black male. His swagger, vivid storytelling, and emotional delivery completely pulled me into the medium that he expressed himself through: hip-hop.

After being heavily intrigued and amazed by rap music, I decided that I wanted to create my own, as it seemed like something I could excel at and use to express myself. Because I found the most comfort in the activities I was praised most highly for, I felt that doing them allowed me to be less inhibited as a black person. I felt that my skin color rendered me so insignificant that there was no reason for me to be around others unless I was doing something worth watching. Rapping appeared to be the coolest thing to do because I had seen those I identified with racially doing it well. I thought I could do well at it too, which would allow me both to express myself fully and to gain social acceptance. Putting my thoughts down on paper allowed me to escape daily reality as a subordinate member of society, and to transform it into a reality in which I held power through my words. I wrote about everything, from my actual life and things I went through to fabricated stories about people in the United States. I enjoyed transcribing my imagination into rap. As I began jotting down my thoughts, feelings, random stories, and even just things that rhymed in cool ways, something was also changing in the social fabric of my peers: being black was becoming cool.

Because gangsta rap, now with 2Pac at the forefront, so heavily influenced popular culture, everything represented and described in this music had become the latest fad to follow for millions of people worldwide who could not relate in the least to being black. The result was that in about 1996, the youth of my hometown, Ballerup, deemed acting like 2Pac the coolest possible behavior: people were imitating the hand signs he was flashing, reciting his lyrics without knowing the true context (or at times even the translation), and trying to dress like they were gangsta rap artists. Everything surrounding the gangsta rap culture became the latest fad. For me, this mainly meant that I could now be comfortable being black. Between 1996 and 1998 I found ways to be a little more comfortable in my skin. I benefited from the social acceptance that popular culture icons whose color matched mine had gained among youth trying to rebel against their parents.

The character traits of the "cool" black people, however, were less than admirable, and my peers began to associate blackness with all these negative qualities. While I was simply looking for a way to feel comfortable by having a point of relation in social situations, I had instead subscribed to perpetuating negative stereotypes by equating the characteristics portrayed in gangsta rap with blackness. Immature and ignorant of the implications, I took comfort in the current trend in my middle school that was pushing me right to the top of the social hierarchy.

The question of whether I was "authentically" black never actually occurred to me because I had no basis for comparison. Because my skin color had caused me so much turmoil and ridicule in my younger years, I clung to the notion that I was black, since it was the only identity I had comfortably adopted. As hip-hop and various other mediums of popular culture set the trends for what was cool and socially coveted, I related many of the hyperbolic images of black masculinity to aspects of my own personality, believing I had found my pathway to fail-safe social acceptance. This type of comfort grew to the point where my personality began to develop into a loud and outrageous character. I sagged, gestured, rapped, and code-switched my way into feeling comfortable in an identity that I saw as a social safety net. Ballerup, Denmark, did not have enough black people for me to understand that what I associated with blackness was not a universal reality. I would eventually realize that even in a community filled with black people, I was outside the norm because of my unique situation growing up.

The turning point of my life came at age twelve, when I was uprooted and had to leave everything I had ever known in Ballerup to move to the United States. My mother had broken up with her boyfriend Jakob two years earlier and now had a fiancé named Enzo. Enzo was a white man of Italian heritage who had grown up in the United States, and my mother decided to follow him overseas to start a new life. Over the next few years our family did quite a bit of moving between different places Enzo had lived before—Philadelphia, Orlando, and then back to Denmark. While these moves taught me to interact with people of all races, it also taught me that I deviated from the norm no matter what type of community I was in. After moving around for a few years, I finally decided that I wanted to move back to Philadelphia to finish high school.

When I was sixteen, I moved in with Enzo's ex-wife, Leslie. Leslie also lived with some of her children by Enzo, who were now my stepsiblings. The house was both crowded and cluttered, a chaotic environment. The three bedrooms and living room were inhabited by as many as nine people, depending on the day and time of year. We also had two flea-infested dogs and an old cat named Missy. For a period of time we also had a friend of the family sleeping in my brother's broken-down Ford Taurus out in front of the house.

Usually someone would be up and using the living room until 3:00 or 4:00 a.m., so I simply had to adapt to noise at all hours of the night. My brothers often had friends coming over very late, and they went in and out of the house to smoke blunts, get drunk, and carry on in the living room. This environment made it very hard to focus on academics and to get a decent night's sleep. My main goals when I moved back to the United States, however, were to earn good grades and finish high school, so I always found a way to get my homework and studying done, even if it meant doing so in a distracting environment. Although I was getting high constantly with one of my stepbrothers, my rule was that I never got high during the week unless I had finished all of my schoolwork. Therefore, the first thing I did when I got home from school was to sit down at the kitchen table and do my homework.

My time back in Philadelphia was also the first time I ever faced challenges to my blackness because of my complexion. As a child, I was always the darkest person around (except for my father), leaving me subject to a variety of jokes regarding how dark I was, how hard I would be to find at night, and so on. In Philadelphia, though, there was a large colored population with a wide range of complexions. During that time I first experienced someone referring to me as "light-skinned." Although I resembled a Negro phenotype, I felt that this comment somehow detracted from the black image I had fabricated and held so dear for most of my life. I had always clung to the notion that I was black, visibly black. If some perceived me as light-skinned, how would that affect my already shaky blackness? Furthermore, because I had grown out my hair during the first few months back in Philadelphia, my status as "other" rather than black in the eyes of others grew. At this point my lack of fashionable apparel, strange demeanor, curly hair, and different vernacular all contributed to what I perceived as the failing of my blackness.

Once again I found myself differing from the norm. The perception of black masculinity I had drawn from my father, *The Fresh Prince*, and 2Pac years earlier seemed obsolete, and I was unable to locate a persona to strive for. Rather than seeing one way a black male should act, I realized that different norms applied to different people. While I wanted to be seen as black in the eyes of my peers, I still did not drastically change my demeanor to fit the norm. I ultimately realized that I would rather be true to myself and strive for my own goals: attending college and succeeding in life. The stereotypical black males at school called me a nerd because I spoke differently and spent class time participating and working.

Living in an area where the complexion and demeanor of the colored population was quite broad allowed me to concern myself less with my complexion. Rather than worrying about looking different, I began to realize that I always stood out in some way, owing to my upbringing. I could relate to many of the people who fit the norm in terms of skin color, but aside from this superficial characteristic, our commonalities varied. Everyone had a different way of dealing with being black in modern society. When color started having less significance in my mind, I was able to concern myself with getting to know myself as a person rather than as "a black person." Although I still wanted to be accepted by my peers and to earn the title of "being black," as I grew I became more concerned with learning about myself as a man than with being among the in-crowd. I felt I was repairing my identity to compensate for the damage caused by all the confusion in my early years. Part of this reparation involved reassessing my relationships with my early black influences and understanding more about their identities. The very first of these influences was my father, and I felt a need to get a deeper understanding of what had shaped the outcome of his life and identity.

Once I finished high school and started college, my father and I did not maintain steady contact. I never really spoke to him over the phone, and he did not have a computer, so we couldn't communicate through email. During my junior year, however, my father sent me a letter. I opened it and immediately was filled with a sense of nostalgia for my childhood. Every birthday and Christmas card had been scribbled in the exact same way—over two entire pages. The penmanship was visibly that of some-one unused to writing, which made sense, considering my father's middle school education. It appeared that he had spent extra time formalizing the letter, skipping every other line to simulate the double spacing in a computer document. Through run-on sentences and poor Danish, I sensed a father's genuine attempt to connect with his son.

About halfway down the first page, he truly tried to reach out to me:

Samiir it's the first time I write to you we have never SpokeN with Eachother as father and son but I think you have dun very WEll I am ProUd over you but one thing I want to say that you should foCus on your sTudies so you can get yourself a good eDucation hope you don't dislike or afTer all these years I should come and decide over you Samiir I write these lines because I want us to start keeping contact by telefone to begin me or that you come n live with me a few days when you come To Denmark we have to start spending time or more specifiCally speak to eachother once a month per Telefone.

While I was reading the letter, tears started streaming down my face. I felt a sense of happiness and pride that my father had reached out in an attempt to connect with me. I saw my father's vulnerability in this letter and began realizing that he did not have all the answers. This was not a man who had been guiding me through black masculinity as a child; this was a man who himself was young when his life had been turned upside down with the sudden responsibility for a life other than his own; a man who in his teens had left everything he had ever known to go live in a for-eign country where he was in the minority. His life and identity as a black man had been shaped by confusion and instability, so for me to base my early identity on his example was illogical. At this point I wanted to see my father as badly as he wished to see me. I wanted to look deeper into his personality and life in order to understand myself better.

The next time I went to Denmark, I lived with my father for most of the time. During this visit I got to spend time with him and see his daily routine of drugs and alcohol. On one occasion I sat down and joined in these activities. It was a Thursday afternoon, and I was sitting around the apartment lounging in my robe. One of my father's friends, who couldn't have been older than twenty-five, came by with a bottle of liquor and immediately began drinking. After about ten minutes, both he and my father snorted a line of amphetamine off the table. Although on some level I felt hurt that my father was living this lifestyle, I also felt a certain sense of connection and pride that our relationship had grown to the point where he would allow me to see this side of him. I poured myself a drink from his friend's bottle of liquor and took a sip. As painful as it was to see his destructive lifestyle, I realized that I could have been in the same position if a couple of circumstances had been different in my life. As we became more and more inebriated, I became increasingly comfortable with seeing and connecting with this side of my father. After about an hour, I joined them as they smoked some hash.

It was three in the afternoon and I was already quite intoxicated. I sat back on the couch, feeling the liquor in my system while listening to my father and his friend converse. Peering through a cloud of hash smoke, I wondered what the two could possibly be speaking about that was of any importance. These were two individuals divided not only by generation but also by race. Were drugs such a point of connection that two individuals from such different walks of life could use them to connect with each other? After pondering this for a few minutes, I realized there must be some sense of kinship around these substances, considering that I was just now connecting with my father at age twenty-one because of them. I felt as if I had been inducted into a fraternity of substance use, sitting there drunk in a hazy room, watching two people of different backgrounds do lines of amphetamine. While it was a strange thing to see, I still felt a sense of resolution in finally being a part of the type of life my father had chosen for so many years over connecting with his family.

I had succeeded in viewing my father just as a person, rather than as the figure who was supposed to teach me how to be black. I was trying to disprove the notion that being black trapped me in a set behavior or thought pattern. This would help me contextualize myself and gain comfort in straying from the norm instead of being depressed by it. I wanted to see myself as black, but I was slowly learning to accept that there was not just one behavioral pattern I had to adhere to. The range of complexions, experiences, and demeanors of black people was vast, and not everyone would stand under the same umbrella. I strove to view people as humans, rather than determining what race they belonged to. The complicated part came when people dictated their behavior on the basis of race and racial stereotypes.

When I first arrived at Dartmouth College, a prestigious liberal arts college in rural New Hampshire, I did not really know what to expect. During the course of my life, I had encountered several different types of black people: people who seemed to subscribe to the stereotypes portrayed on television, and people who were black but had nothing to do with the stereotypes on television. I wondered what types of people I would encounter at Dartmouth.

What I found in college was that not many people shared the "black" experience in terms of what it stereotypically implies: lower socioeconomic status, an urban environment, and so on. If the aforementioned implied anything about blackness, then I found that I, in fact, would seem to be one of the blackest people at the school. I did not fully subscribe to the stereotypical behavior that accompanies such experiences, because I was growing accustomed to concerning myself with my natural inclinations rather than adhering to how people expected me to act. Much as I had determined in high school, there were certain types of behaviors that signified "blackness." It was my assumption, however, that those who subscribed to these behaviors did so because of their life experiences. My assumption turned out to be incredibly wrong; it seemed that many of the black people at Dartmouth who acted "black" appeared to do so in order to legitimize their blackness. Many of them used inner-city slang, wore urban attire, and generally had an inner-city demeanor. My impression was that these people were trying to establish a new identity while at college—one they hadn't had access to in high school. Perhaps they had been like me, considered nerds because they weren't black enough, and were now trying to escape that label. The difference between them and me, however, was that I had actually lived many of the experiences that created these signifiers of an authentic black experience. I simply chose not to act them out because I was finding comfort in straying from the norm and focusing more on myself.

Because of the way I perceived many of the black people at my college, I continued to be somewhat of a loner. I had friends, but I did not let too many people get close to me. We were at a privileged school like Dartmouth, so why would they want to hear about the drug charges my brother back home was facing, my father's drug problem, or my family's money problems? I did not disclose much information about these things because I figured people would place me in the same box with many of the other black people at Dartmouth, assuming I was disclosing these things only to legitimize some form of blackness related to the struggles commonly faced in urban environments.

I found that those I got along with best were those who did not concern themselves too much with how they were perceived by others, but rather were true to themselves and simply focused on enjoying college and getting an education. My diverse life experience had finally made me as close to color-blind as one can be, and I selected my friends entirely because of their demeanor, and in no way for their skin color or social class. As I grew more comfortable at Dartmouth, I began to understand the value of my life experience more fully. All of the places I had lived and all my struggles had made me a person who could relate to and communicate with almost anyone, no matter where a person was from.

Just as blacks had been portrayed in their first cinematic representation in *Birth of a Nation* as lazy, good-for-nothing slackers, many blacks at Dartmouth would try to embody this stereotype in an effort to claim their blackness. Rather than bragging about who had the best grades or who performed best under pressure, many conversations would lead to a competition over who could convince the other that he was a worse student—whether these claims were true or not. Realizing this, I became comfortable with what I was and whom I had become for one of the first times in my life. Not only had my unique and incredibly diverse life experience helped me adapt to college and gain acceptance from my peers and interest from my professors, but also it embodied the struggles that so many black students for some reason wished they had experienced, which gave me further legitimization in the eyes of those who actually gauged this as something important.

While I was thankful I had endured the circumstances I had, I would never want to do that again. When I was embarrassed because my family did not have as much money as others or when I had to see family members deal with substance abuse, the last thing I thought about was how it might legitimize me at a later point; all I wanted was to overcome it. Once I finally made something out of myself and matriculated at an Ivy League school, my previous struggles and failures became marks of pride as opposed to points of shame.

I have been called "nigger," been on the receiving end of racial jokes, and struggled with my own self-worth solely because of my skin color. Regardless of how strange I seem to my peers and how little I fall within the scope of stereotypical blackness, my life and identity have been dramatically influenced by my complexion. How could anyone tell me that I am not black? Limiting blackness to a number of stereotypes and negative behaviors is ignorant and disrespectful to the race as a whole. So while I consider myself black (well, half black), I will never again allow this label to dictate the way I interact with others or present myself to the outside world. At times it will change how I am perceived and treated, but as a man who has endured this label my entire life, I shall not let myself be affected. Through the same actions, thoughts, and expressions that make me so hard to define, I will continue to prove to those around me that it is best to define me by my character and not my complexion.

Upon graduating from Dartmouth College, Samiir accepted a position as a marketing strategist with a leading agency. After arriving at what he considers a place of peace and stability, Samiir has started the long process of getting his father clean from substance abuse.

III

A DIFFERENT PERSPECTIVE

9

Taica Hsu   Chow Mein Kampf

While attending my predominantly white elementary school, I did my best to fit in by acting white—speaking English without an accent, having white friends, and wearing "normal" clothing. Even though I looked different from most of my classmates, I never felt different, at least in terms of race. I always had friends, and my academic ability was never attributed to my race.

My third-grade teacher, Mrs. Dali, gave us a quiz every week to test our knowledge of the times tables. Wayne, a white classmate, and I consistently finished first and second, making no errors. For some reason I became known as the "Human Calculator," and Wayne was simply my competition.

"Wayne, how did you do on the eights?"
"I think I got most of them right. How about you?"
"Yeah, me too. It was a little harder than the sixes or the sevens."
"Yeah, but we always finish first."

While I enjoyed the title, I never thought it was due to my being Chinese, or that I was expected to be better at math because I was Asian. My affinity for numbers followed me throughout elementary school, earning me blue ribbons in various math competitions and a plaque for first place in Superstars, a monthly worksheet of challenging math problems that was given to all students.

In fifth grade, my teacher recognized my passion for mathematics and nominated me for the gifted students program. I skipped almost six hours of regular class per week to spend time with similar students, studying topics such as the rainforest and chaos theory. My teacher expected us to embrace new forms of learning and assessed our performance through skits, plays, simulations, and Toastmasters, a program that enhances public-speaking skills. We were also expected to keep up with regular coursework. Consequently, I developed a special identity—that of one who deserved to skip regular classes to fraternize with the elite. That identity was shattered on the very first day of gifted class.

The students around me were capable of handling metaphor, representation, and, above all, creativity. I was not. Or perhaps I was just too shy, too insecure to share a novel response with the class. Whatever the reason, I left the teacher unimpressed, frustrated, and skeptical about my special placement in the class. Failure was a hard pill to swallow, and it left me vulnerable. In an all-white class of gifted and talented students, my race became a salient factor for the first time in my life. Why can everyone else see the fishing hole when I can't? Why can everyone else deliver a public speech confidently when I can't? I searched for an explanation for my obvious differences from the rest of "the club." Naturally, I blamed my race. After all, Asians were supposed to be good at math but also timid, shy, and less outgoing than their white counterparts. Although I was not as hyperaware of these stereotypes in fifth grade as I am now, I do remember feeling different because of my physical appearance and linking that difference with my failures in the gifted class. I allowed my own internalized racism to stunt my growth as an individual: instead of working hard to improve my speaking ability and my facility with words, I figured I would never be as good as others when it came to verbalizing my thoughts and chose instead to focus on my strengths.

What perhaps sets my experience apart from that of monoracial individuals is the fact that I questioned why I didn't have the best of both worlds. If I am half white and half Asian, why shouldn't I be good at math *and* creative and outgoing? Since we cannot pick and choose the genes we get from our parents, I figured my Asian side dominated my white side. I used this hypothesis to explain my physical attributes as well, since most people thought I looked more Asian than white. I despised this notion, perhaps even more than I rejected my timidity. People can't tell by looking at you that you're an introvert, but race is there for everyone to see.

Middle school proved to be slightly better, at least in terms of racial diversity. I continued in the gifted program, which was now a completely separate team, so all of the students who were sorted to the top traveled together. While I am not a proponent of tracking in schools, I must say the environment was extremely conducive to learning. As many more races were represented in the classroom, I began to broaden my definition of what it meant to be "gifted."

Although I do not remember meeting other Asians, I did meet the first person my age that I knew was also biracial, half African American and half white. We started dating in seventh grade, perhaps more because of peer pressure than physical attraction. As I look back, I remember being enamored of the attention and the social status that accompanies dating an attractive and popular girl. Hidden beneath the surface, however, was the lingering fear that this wasn't for me.

McKayla identified more strongly with her African American side and sometimes complained about her "light skin." Most of her closest friends were full African American, but for some reason she had a thing for a half-Asian boy who was shorter than her and obviously less developed. During our three-month relationship, I felt puny and, quite frankly, emasculated. McKayla was much taller, had large breasts, and typically attracted jocks who were much taller and more masculine than me. At one point she even told one of my best friends—Jamison, a muscular jock who hung out with me in private, but never during school—that I didn't have much pubic hair. Ironically, it was with Jamison that I shared my first homosexual experience. It shouldn't be surprising, then, that when I found out a year later that Jamison and McKayla were dating, I was more envious of McKayla than of Jamison.

Recently, through Facebook, I reconnected with McKayla and discovered that she too has had homosexual relationships. Although she identifies as bisexual, I find it intriguing that our union was not the match either of us really wanted. We laughed and joked that if middle-schoolers were more accepting of same-sex relationships, perhaps both of us would have come out earlier.

Jamison came over almost every weekend for sleepovers. One night, he initiated a conversation about a long pillow he found in my room.

"What do you use this for?"

"Sometimes I sleep with it at night," I replied.

"I have an idea. Let's put it between us and pretend we are each other's girl-friend," Jamison suggested.

I was excited and petrified at the same time. *Does he want to have sex? What if my parents hear us? Does he want to be my boyfriend? I'd better lock the door.*

Jamison and I dry-humped the pillow for thirty minutes, continuously moaning our girlfriends' names. *McKayla. Katie. McKayla. Katie.* The interactions intensified with future sleepovers until there was no longer a need for the cotton barrier.

"Do you want to do the pillow thing?" Jamison asked.
"Sure," I replied, already with a slight erection.

That night I performed oral sex on him and I remember thinking, "Does this mean I'm gay?"

And so I added one more item to the "being half Asian" list: slow sexual and physical development (but not homosexuality). It was becoming clear that my racial background was more a curse than a blessing. Jamison was white, and also taller, stronger, more attractive, and better equipped (so to speak) than me. He represented the standard of male beauty and behavior, even though he engaged in sexual activity with other males behind the scenes. Jamison also could easily cover his homosexual tendencies—or "curiosities," as he liked to say—since he acted and talked like a typical male. I, by contrast, had a higher voice, a smaller body, and the stereotypical mannerisms that society attributes to gay men. These characteristics were beginning to manifest themselves more and more as the middle school years passed by, and more and more people began to notice. Therefore, my Asian side not only stunted my development but also prevented me from hiding my true sexuality for a longer period of time.

In retrospect, I believe that Jamison and I interpreted our activities behind closed doors in different ways. Although I eagerly anticipated his embrace, I felt that he used our escapades simply for sexual pleasure. After he got off, he was done. I always wanted more—affection, attention, time to cuddle. He wanted to sleep. I doubt that Jamison cried for hours like me after we missed the chance to say good-bye before I moved to California. I doubt that he desperately searched for my lingering scent when he returned home. I doubt that he waited by the phone every weekend in anticipation of the next sleepover. Jamison was my first love; I was his "experiment."

Years later, during the summer of my sophomore year in high school, Jamison admitted that he frequently participated in threesomes with both girls and guys. *Was he gay too?* I pondered this for years. To this day, I have no idea where Jamison stands in terms of his sexuality. My best guess is that he plays the part of a heterosexual white male quite well and sleeps with men on the side. I must admit, I used to covet his chameleon-like identity—what Kenji Yoshino, a gay, half-Japanese Yale law professor, aptly calls "covering." As always, I blamed my Asian genes for my inability to float through society unnoticed: that small, femme Asian boy must be gay. *Why can't I be Jamison? Why can't I just sleep with other men?* Thankfully, although I was tortured by such thoughts as a teen, today I wear the pink triangle with pride as an ambassador of the gay community.

My family decided to move to California when I was fourteen years old, the summer after I graduated from eighth grade. After shoving the last box into the back of my mom's black Bronco, I sat in the passenger seat with tears in my eyes. My mom and I waved good-bye to my sister and my dad as I left my childhood in the dust. Jamison was supposed to visit me the night before, but he failed to show, which intensified my depression. I cried for hours in my closet, a prisoner of my own sexuality.

Our move to California was not optional. Five years earlier, my father had secretly started gambling large amounts of money at a nearby racetrack. After discovering a racing receipt in his back pocket, my mom hired a private detective to monitor his behavior. But it was too late. My father had already tapped into our family savings, lost it all, taken out a second mortgage, and, to top it off, refused to collect money from his lucrative construction jobs. With debt accruing and nearly no income, my mom and I were forced to move in with my great-grandmother, who lived three thousand miles away.

My mom had her own way of describing my father's financial irresponsibility: "If I were standing outside in the freezing cold and one of your father's friends was also outside, your father would give his jacket to his friend." I once thought that the crude metaphor meant my father did not love my mom. I realized years later that what she meant was that my father has a lot of pride and, knowing that his family would always love him, needed to appear strong and generous to those on the outside—friends, employers, business partners—at the expense of his family. My mom attributed this to my father's Chinese heritage, claiming that gambling was rampant in Asian communities. I, however, question whether this was the cause: my father could have been from any racial background and still have developed a gambling addiction. What I view as the most characteristically Asian of my father's actions throughout this scandal was his complete lack of emotion, which is precisely what I blamed for my failure in the gifted class. He never expressed sorrow or remorse for his actions and appeared entirely unaffected by our forced move to California. I must have inherited my father's indifferent attitude toward life's obstacles, which would explain my decision to focus on my strengths (mathematics and logical reasoning) and to abandon my weaknesses (language arts and public speaking).

I knew my dad was wrong, but even to this day I have never heard the slightest admission of guilt, or even a simple "I'm sorry." Thus, the tension between our family cultures intensified even further. My white mom wore her emotions on her sleeve and explained, with considerable remorse, the events that necessitated uprooting our life. My Chinese dad never said a word about the situation, at least to me. He said he would stay in Florida, take care of things, and meet us in California. Simple. It shouldn't be surprising, then, that he was the only one with dry eyes when our family split.

Watching my parents deal with their emotions in such different ways made being white more attractive to me. I did not enjoy suppressing my emotions, particularly those related to my secret sexual identity. Yet I felt confined by my Chinese dad's approach to emotion: keep it in, don't talk about it, hide it. Why couldn't I be more like my white mom and share my true feelings? If both my parents were white, would coming out have been easier, less taboo? I suppose gender roles added another layer of confusion to an already complex situation. Society characterizes men as emotionless and rational, women as irrationally emotional. Therefore, I question whether my dad adheres more strongly to the male or the Asian stereotype. Both identities certainly contribute to his inability to accept my identity as a gay, biracial male. Lest I shame my father even more, I relegated my emotions to the confines of the same closet that had, until high school, successfully concealed my sexuality.

Attending a new high school in a different state exacerbated the biracial duality that first reared its ugly head in the academic arena. As I traveled from class to class, I wove in and out of older students who towered over me. Once again I felt puny, underdeveloped, and, this time, insignificant. The other Asian students I passed stood at eye level, which prompted me to identify more strongly with my Asian side, at least in terms of physical attributes. My behavior in the classroom could also be characterized as stereotypically Asian: I listened intently to the teacher, never said anything unsolicited, and consistently completed all of my schoolwork. The identity conflict emerged when I went home to my white mom and great-grandmother. Both of them have blond hair and blue-green eyes, and my dark brown hair and milk chocolate eyes occasionally produced the suspicion that I was adopted. To complicate matters further, we lived in California for two years without my father, the only real connection I ever had to my Asian heritage. As a result, the layers of white got thicker and thicker.

My father's absence and his life-changing financial blunders, coupled with my dependency on my white family members, eventually severed my will to self-identify as Asian. The choice, however, was not conscious; I only began to acknowledge my self-loathing behaviors after almost two years of college. I took every opportunity in high school to correct people: "No, I'm not Asian. I'm *half* Asian." On surveys and standardized tests, I checked "white" if no "biracial" option was available. When I spent time with my Asian friends, I found solace in the fact that I looked different and reasoned that since I was half white, the traditional standard of beauty, I was more attractive. As a twisted consequence, I started to surround myself with more and more Asian friends, most of them female. It was easy to do, since my Advanced Placement and International Baccalaureate classes were predominantly white and Asian. Whenever I hung out with Asians, I would reject their Asian features and think (to myself, of course) that I could never be attracted to an Asian person. My early dating habits would reflect this belief.

The layers of being gay and white grew thicker when I joined the swim team my sophomore year. Swimming is not the most masculine sport, but with the tight Speedos and fit male bodies, I could live out my fantasies under the guise of athleticism and boosting my résumé for college applications. While changing and showering, I had to conceal my ever-growing attraction for Brandyn, a teammate who was a year older. Brandyn, who identified as black, was much taller and better endowed than me (this was becoming a pattern, much to my disappointment). We became close friends very quickly, which became evident to those around us, and they questioned our sexuality: "Are you and Brandyn boyfriends? You hang out all the time." Although we repeatedly denied it, I secretly wanted a boyfriend and dreamed that Brandyn would be my first.

One night, in the middle of one of our many phone conversations, I decided to reveal one of my darkest secrets for the first time.

"So, I've done stuff with guys before. My friend and I had sleepovers and we used to play around."

"Really? Me too," Brandyn replied calmly, with a hint of surprise and excitement in his voice.

"Cool. With who?" I inquired, now with a slight erection.

"One of my best friends in middle school."

"That's pretty much when Jamison and I started out. We fooled around but
never had real sex," which to me at that time meant anal intercourse.

It felt so good to get that off my chest, especially with someone who
shared a similar experience. Unfortunately, I still needed to defend my
sexuality.

"I still like girls, but it was fun to fool around with a guy."
"Yeah, same here," Brandyn agreed.
"Have you ever had real sex with a guy?"
"Nope. Never. It could be fun, though."

As this point my erection was rock hard, and somehow I knew that
Brandyn would be my first. I was scared, though. Did this mean I was really gay? What if I still got turned on by girls? Whenever I masturbated, I
always thought about boys; the same was true of porn. It seemed that the
more "gay" things I did, the closer I got to actually being gay. This was
not what either of my parents had planned, especially my father, who I
knew desperately wanted me to raise a son of my own. He reminded me of
this fact when he reentered my life toward the end of my sophomore year
to open a Chinese restaurant less than a mile from where we lived. It was
a full house—me, my mom, my father, and my great-grandma packed into
a tiny one-bedroom. My desperate need for privacy would soon reveal my
darkest secret.

Brandyn and I hung out at his place two days after the memorable
phone call. We were alone, sitting on his bed and contemplating whether
or not we should go into the closet and fool around. Funny that we were
already "in the closet" and yet felt the need to go into a real one to act on
our sexual desires. After ten minutes of flirtatious debate, we entered the
closet in his bedroom, and thus began my relationship with my first true
boyfriend.

Brandyn and I continued to fool around into my junior year of high
school. We took advantage of our parents' work schedules and alternated
houses so as not to arouse suspicion. One day after school I invited Brandyn to my house, anticipating that my parents would not be home until
10:00 p.m., after the Chinese restaurant closed. This would give us plenty
of time to mess around and get rid of any evidence—lube, condoms, rum-
pled sheets. After having sex in my bed, we fell asleep in each other's arms.
Although I remember hearing the outer metal door open and a key being
inserted into the inner door, I was still half asleep and too unconscious to

react. Brandyn and I opened our eyes and saw my father staring at us from no more than fifteen feet away.

"Get out of my house!" he yelled, pointing to the door.

Before I had time to say anything, Brandyn slipped past my father and out the door. My father left shortly thereafter without acknowledging me at all, and we would never speak of what he had seen until my sophomore year of college, more than three years later. I remember being less worried about my father's reaction than about Brandyn's well-being. Since this was before the viral presence of cell phones, I did the only thing I could do: I drove to Brandyn's house, hoping that I would find him walking home. Sure enough, I saw him walking along a busy street, made a U-turn, and picked him up. On the way to his house, we discussed how frightened we were and whether or not this meant we would have to end our relationship. Although we assured each other that it would not, social pressures would eventually bring my first gay relationship to an end.

Brandyn and I spent less and less time together, even though we continued to have sex until my sophomore year of college. We agreed to stop dating because of the enormous pressure we felt from living at home and being in the closet. As despicable as it sounds, I became embarrassed and uncomfortable around Brandyn during my junior year and his final year of high school. I would avoid him during lunch and engage in only limited conversation during swim practice. Although part of me missed him during my senior year, I was relieved to know that the only other classmate who knew I was gay no longer attended my school. In an effort to suppress my homosexuality even more, I fabricated a crush on a Korean girl who was part of my cohort of friends. I knew I was lying to her, myself, and Brandyn, but this was the only way I knew to get rid of being gay.

Melisa and I were friends throughout high school and shared many of the same friends. She was full Korean, and the differences between us in terms of Asian influence were obvious. Melisa spoke Korean at home with both of her parents and her brother, and they ate traditional Korean food almost every night. She also attended a church with a congregation that was almost entirely Asian. Socially, Melisa was held to stricter rules, especially when it came to dating. Although her parents never knew we were romantically involved, Melisa warned that they would be devastated and disapproving if they found out, because I was not Korean. Her father was apparently very traditional when it came to dating and marriage and refused to acknowledge any suitor who was not Korean.

Getting insights into Melisa's full-Asian life reaffirmed the benefits of being only half Asian. My parents never mandated racial parameters for my partners, although it *was* assumed that I would date and marry a woman. I could negotiate my curfew and never had to speak in anything but English. Lastly—and this is something for which I still feel guilty—I had only one parent whose accent caused me embarrassment and, to some extent, shame. Melisa's parents both had heavy accents and spoke limited English in my presence. Although I never broached the subject with her, I always wondered if she shared my sense of humiliation when introducing her parents to native English speakers. I took comfort in the fact that my white mother participated more frequently than my father in school functions and was often the first of my parents to meet my friends.

Melisa and I dated during the last few months of my senior year of high school and into the summer, right before I left for college. A bunch of my friends, all of whom were white, Asian, or a combination of the two, slept over the night before I left for college. We drove to the airport in a caravan of three vehicles, crying the entire way while listening to a CD of our favorite songs. Before ascending the escalator past the airport checkpoint, I hugged each of my friends, shielding the depth of my sadness behind my dark sunglasses—a technique I probably picked up from my father. Melisa was last, and as she gingerly lifted the sunglasses from my eyes, she sighed, "You can't hide your true feelings from me." We kissed, and she sent me off with a ten-page handwritten letter about how our love would never end and how we would remain close, despite the three thousand miles between Los Angeles and my college in New England. The irony was that I cried more for Shawn, my half-Thai, half-white friend, with whom I had shared another scintillating homosexual experience that summer.

During high school, when I had noticed I was mostly in the company of Asians, I also became hyperaware of the number of boys and girls in our group of friends. I was always more satisfied when the boys outnumbered the girls; more testosterone, of course, helped to confirm my heterosexuality. Shawn, who was the only boy at my eighteenth birthday party, asked me, "What other boys do you hang out with?" I could tell that he was anxious about the idea that he was my closest guy friend, especially with rumors circulating that I was gay. Perhaps he could also tell that I had a huge crush on him.

Shawn and I became friends in the middle of our junior year of high school. I secretly wanted Shawn during the entire time that I dated Melisa, which led to my infidelity the summer before I left for college. Shawn's family invited me on a month-long trip to Germany, which would have been financially impossible if they had not offered to pay for everything except the plane ticket. Shawn's wealth attracted me, particularly because my family had struggled financially. My grandparents surprised me with a plane ticket as a graduation gift, and with that I was off on my next gay adventure. I remember feeling torn about the fact that Shawn was Asian. For so long I had rejected Asian characteristics, and now I was lusting after someone with those very features. Shawn, however, was tall and only half Asian, which I convinced myself attracted me more than a full Asian would. He also was one of the few guys with whom I was close.

During the trip we stayed at the home of Shawn's relatives. For the first few nights Shawn and I slept apart, but eventually we started sharing a bed. Every night before we fell asleep, I would gradually inch closer and closer to Shawn's side of the bed—first my hand, then my foot, then my entire leg. After a few days I took a chance. One night, when I thought Shawn was asleep, I ran my fingers across his face and over his lips. No response. I did it again. No response. I continued caressing his face until he finally said, "What are you doing?"

"Does it feel good?" I responded gently.
"Yeah, kinda. But it's kinda weird."
"Let me know when you want me to stop," I suggested coyly.

Shawn said nothing else and we fell asleep, our bodies touching.

Although Shawn ejaculated twice by my hand that summer, there was absolutely no reciprocation, and he maintained that he was straight. Regardless of his sexual orientation, I knew that I was succumbing to my sexual desires and enjoying it. I no longer talk to Shawn, but I've caught myself wondering on occasion if he too struggled with a gay, half-Asian identity.

I traveled to college with my father, the parent who knew the least about me and the least about American culture. Since I was attending an Ivy League school, my father thought I would have to wear a suit to every lecture. (Any student who has worn sweatpants to class knows this is certainly not the case.) We discussed our competing views about and expectations for college while we shopped for the typical items—bathroom supplies, clothes, and gear for my upcoming freshman canoeing trip—and the not-so-typical items that my father insisted we purchase: a rice cooker, yellow medicine, dried squid, and a bamboo plant for good luck. Although I protested briefly, it was these very items that made me feel the most at home while acclimating to college life.

My dad and I met my first classmate in the elevator of the Hanover Inn. Naomi, who was African American, was traveling with both of her parents, who were dressed very formally and spoke English without an accent. The fact that all three were significantly taller than my dad and me exacerbated the differences I perceived in our socioeconomic status: Naomi's parents appeared well educated, while neither of my parents had graduated from college; both of Naomi's parents accompanied her to college, while my mom stayed at home because of financial constraints. I exited the elevator wondering how I would fit in as a biracial gay student from a less affluent background. There had to be others like me, right?

The next student my father and I encountered was my freshman roommate, Damien, a white boy from upstate New York. He too had traveled with both his parents, who also were nicely dressed and appeared well educated. After most of the parents left, my roommate and I quickly became friends with another set of roommates on the same floor, Wanda and Paige, who were both Asian. We ate meals together, studied in the common room, attended frat parties, and even went on road trips, all before the spring of our freshman year. Although we were close, I was still hiding the biggest part of my identity.

One night in the spring, when the snow had already melted, I walked into Wanda's room wearing a T-shirt and mesh shorts and lay down next to her in bed. This was typical of our relationship, and there was never any sexual tension—obviously. Lying next to Wanda was comfortable, and by that time I considered her my best friend at college. Eventually she would become my best straight friend. After about fifteen minutes of cuddling, I initiated the most important conversation of my life, which lasted less than sixty seconds.

"Wanda, what do you think of bisexual people?"
"Um, I don't know."
"Do you think it's weird...or wrong?"
"No, I don't think so."
"Okay. I think I'm bisexual."
"Okay."

At the time I think I anticipated a more dramatic reaction, for better or worse: "Oh my God, no way!" "Really? That's great!" "Kiss me and prove it." Regardless of what I thought would happen, Wanda's reaction was perfect for me at that moment in my coming-out story. She didn't change her tone of voice, she didn't distance herself from me on the bed, she didn't judge, and, best of all, our relationship only grew stronger. Wanda gave me the confirmation I needed that being gay was okay. Her choice of words sent that very message.

I returned home the summer after my freshmen year and saw old friends, including Brandyn and Melisa. I came out to a group of ten friends at the same time and used the story about Shawn and Brandyn to make the process a little more comforting. Once again, my friends were overwhelmingly supportive and, to be honest, not surprised. I confided in them that telling my parents would be far more difficult. A few of my Asian friends even posited that my dad would be the hardest to tell. It turned out they were right.

I came out to my parents over winter break during my first year at college. One night I told my dad I was going to hang out with Brandyn, to which he retorted, "He's weird. I don't want you to see him." In the back of my mind I knew he could not escape the image of me and Brandyn in bed together. It tore him up inside, but he did not have the courage or the words to express how he truly felt. So I did it for him.

"You know what, Dad, I'm gay!"
"No, you're not!"

My mom walked in from her room. "What did you say?" she inquired, half asleep.

"I'm gay. And Dad doesn't want me to see Brandyn, but I'm going anyway."

My parents walked out to the backyard in silence, and I could hear their subsequent conversation.

"How could you let him be like this?" my father said, jabbing at my mom.
"I had no idea, Stan."
"He's not gay. I'll take him to a strip club and prove it."

For the next three years, my father's parting words every time I left for college were not "I love you" but "Make the right decisions." I knew exactly what he was referring to, but the word "gay" never came out of his mouth after that historic night. Eventually he stopped asking about my love life, and he stills lives in complete denial about my identity. My mom, by contrast, is extremely supportive. Throughout my college years, she would call and tell me about the latest LGBTQ drama she watched on

Lifetime, meanwhile crying over the phone. My mom and my sister are the only family members who have met any of my significant others. My Chinese family still thinks I will get married to a beautiful girl and, they hope, have a boy to continue my father's bloodline.

I graduated from college with a newfound sense of self, a respect for my own sexuality, and a burgeoning desire to make the world a safer place for LGBTQ youth. For the first time in my life, I made gay friends with whom I was open, comfortable, and real, and for the first time, the world saw the real me.

I currently teach high school math in San Francisco. Although I was hesitant to come out to my students during my first year of teaching, I have since become the adviser to the Gay-Straight Alliance, and I now come out to all my classes every year. While I forget exactly what it felt like to be in the closet, I can certainly empathize with students who fear being "outed." My goal is to make school a safe space for students to reveal their identities without any repercussions. Who knew that the scrawny, half-Asian boy who dated girls would become a gay advocate?

I still struggle with the perception of my race in the gay male community and my own attraction to full-Asian gay men. Homophobia certainly exists within LGBTQ spaces and manifests itself in gay men as the desire to date only "masculine men." Asian men are stereotyped as having more feminine characteristics, and thus we often feel emasculated—exactly how I felt next to McKayla—and viewed as less desirable by some gay men. As a result, I have become hypersensitive to the reasons why gay men are or are not attracted to me: Do they like me because I am exotic (half Asian)? Do they not like me because I look too Asian? How do I cover my more effeminate (read: Asian) characteristics and features? I am still haunted by my childhood desire to look more white and to differentiate myself from my full-Asian counterparts. I hope to overcome these hurdles in time and fully accept my mixed racial background. Then, and only then, will my gay identity and racial identity truly exist in harmony.

After graduating from Dartmouth, Taica received his Master's from Stanford University and currently teaches in a high school in San Francisco. As faculty adviser to the Gay-Straight Alliance, he works to create a safe space for all LGBTQ youth and their allies. Taica is an advocate for social justice in schools. He dresses in drag to combat homophobia and heteronormativity while educating youth about the differences between gender and sexual orientation.

10

By Anise Vance   A Work in Progress

The small fictions I play with are often more plausible than my true history. When I am asked "Where are you from?" the conversation that ensues can last hours. I am poked and prodded as if I were a physical specimen of twentieth-century globalization. Sometimes it is just easier to say that I am from Santa Fe.

My father is African American, born and bred in Hartford, Connecticut. He has the thick American accent of a Yankee broadcaster and speaks carefully, precisely, and authoritatively. He dons suits and ties now, but a college photo shows him sporting an Afro, a dashiki, and the wide smile of someone having a good deal of fun. He still wears the large square glasses popular in the 1970s, which somehow suited him, with his graying moustache and bald head. He is deeply intelligent, incredibly hardworking, wonderfully wise, and a devoted father.

Born in Iran, my mother left her home country in her early twenties to study in Boston. She describes her youthful self as a fiery liberal who defied conservative Persian norms and lived life to the fullest. By all accounts, my mom was a heartbreaker; when I was in my teens, I caught snippets of a conversation between her and an old friend about love letters some hapless suitor had penned to her when they were in college. Her voice has the elegant lilt of a poet and traces of Farsi cadences. Watching her work a room is unnerving; she wins people's affections like the Romans conquered the West. At my mother's core resides a certain toughness—a trait common among the women in my family—fortified by intelligence and understanding. Wrap that in a whole lot of love, empathy, and creativity, and *voilà*, you have my mom.

My mother never planned on living in the United States permanently. My dad's marriage proposal was vague at best: "Would you mind delaying going overseas for a few years?" After a couple of days, when he finally asked her directly to marry him, she replied that she thought she had already said yes. And so it was that the confusion surrounding my family began well before I was born.

My parents' first stop after college was Abidjan, Côte d'Ivoire, where they arrived with my older sister, an excitable and beautiful baby. Three years later my family was treated to a special delight: I was born, cross-eyed, yellow with jaundice, and troublingly sleepy. I remember nothing of my time in Côte d'Ivoire; we moved when I was one year old to Nairobi, Kenya, where we would spend the next seven years. It was in Kenya that I learned to read, ride a bike, and play sports. We had three dogs—Nero, Meshki, and Heidi—and a basketball hoop. I loved school, loved my friends, and loved coming home to run around with the dogs. I would often beg my sister, whom I worshipped, for the tiniest scrap of affection. Life was blissful, and I knew who I was: a Kenyan.

I was eight when the carpet was pulled out from under me and we moved to Botswana. There I attended British schools that demanded military-like discipline. I was heartbroken at leaving Nairobi. I missed our dogs, my sister was going through a moody puberty, and the upheaval in general left me grumpy. I did find comfort in the friendship of two fellow Iranians. We would play cops and robbers, shouting *"Khomeini omahd"* (Khomeini has come) at the top of our lungs, and attended Farsi classes on the weekends. We idolized the older Persian boys, with their slick facial hair and off-color jokes, and nurtured crushes on the pretty Iranian girls. I still described myself as Kenyan, but others called me American and "colored," a term often used in southern Africa to describe people with brown skin. I accepted both identities nonchalantly because they mattered little to me. To my mind I was somewhere between Kenyan and Iranian.

Three years after so abruptly moving to Kenya, my family once again picked up and shipped out. Cairo, Egypt, was to be our last stop in Africa and the city where I would complete middle and high school. On the Cairene streets I discovered that, to many Egyptians, I looked like one of them. Among the first and most necessary words I learned were *"Mish aref Arabe"* (I don't understand Arabic). At the international school I attended, I was considered American because I spoke no Arabic, had my father's thick Yankee accent, and was unacquainted with Egyptian culture. I was, however, also completely unfamiliar with mainstream American norms. I was an outsider to both the Egyptians and the Americans who attended my school. My closest friends shared my outsider status: we were the black kids.

This Thing Called Blackness

In middle school, my best friend was a dark-skinned Egyptian American who readily identified as black. God, how we "black kids" loved race. I remember the nights we spent pretending to be stand-up comedians, using "negro" and "nigger" as punch lines. Like most boys our age, we obsessed over sports and girls while awakening to music and fashion. Predictably, we wore baggy clothing, tried out various neck chains, and drooled over all-white sneakers. Our musical tastes evolved from Nelly's party hip-hop to the socially conscious work of Mos Def and Talib Kweli (a.k.a. Black Star). Without truly understanding the meaning of the rhymes, I memorized verse after verse. As we moved from mimicking shallow stereotypes to the very beginnings of comprehension, the word "nigger" held a place of particular import. It was something we uttered only around one another and with specific intent. We felt that using it made us part of a world where we weren't held at arm's length. We were brothers, and there were legions of us.

"Nigger" became our special code word. It took me years to use it in front of a white person, and I clearly remember the first time I did so:

Paul (who was black):   "No, man, this is the nigger couch."
David (who was white):   "Huh?"
Me: "Yah, man, nigger couch."

As the word tumbled out of my mouth, it felt heavy, bloated, and out of place. It was the first and last time I would say the word "nigger" in the presence of a white person, and also the last time I would use it in front of Paul.

Paul arrived in tenth grade, a military kid from Hattiesburg, Mississippi. Paul and his brother, Dejuan, quickly became my closest friends. Paul was razor smart and viciously determined. His stern attitude made him both feared and admired. Dejuan, meanwhile, was a jokester who could charm water from a rock. He was rarely seen without a grin and never without a girl. And, yes, my two best friends were black. The three of us happened to be the only black Americans in our class that year.

I felt at home with them, despite our enormous differences. My American family hailed from the North, as Paul and Dejuan would often remind me, while theirs was rooted in the South. They were staunch Christians while I was born into a Baha'i family. Both their parents were black; I was mixed. But in the dog-eat-dog world that is high school, you need people you can trust. We never felt the need to find an army of folk like us, and for me, our friendship was liberating: I no longer needed to rely on black stereotypes—or to use the word that I thought came with that—to belong and to bond. Race may have been the original reason for our friendship, but it was not what kept us friends. We simply liked, believed in, and trusted one another.

When we graduated from high school, Paul and Dejuan enrolled in the Naval Academy, while I was lucky enough to go to Dartmouth College in New Hampshire. Culture shock does not even begin to describe my first impressions of that school. It was a freakishly foreign land to me. Unlike in the countries of my upbringing, white folk were everywhere at Dartmouth, fraternities and sororities were the major social centers, and no one seemed to know the first thing about hummus or shawarma. I was not alone in my feelings of alienation; in that supposed wonderland of privilege, a lot of young people got lost.

Let us be frank: college is a circus. Groups of friends are shaped and re-shaped constantly, people fall in and out of love in a heartbeat, and everyone freaks out when—boom!—four years are quickly up and we discover that we still know next to nothing about ourselves or the world. I am still trying to work out what happened at college.

For starters, I dove into the black community through various campus organizations. I served on our black student union's executive board and on the Inter-Community Council. I was an advocate for issues affecting the black community and helped found a group for men of color on campus. I wrote my thesis on segregated black populations and spent a good deal of my time railing about inequality. Issues of race were, clearly, at the forefront of my mind. Yet despite the public face I showed on campus, it was in the most private sphere that I took another step forward in understanding my mixed identity.

During my junior year I took a course on interracial intimacy. During a discussion on the relevance of mixed-race interactions to racial progress, one young woman remarked, "The key question is who is in your bed." She was making a simple point: intimacy, which is not synonymous with sex, is the final test of prejudice. Many students in the class shifted uncomfortably. I was involved with black and nonblack women during college. My two most serious relationships were with a white woman, Mary, and a Native American woman, Annette. Mary once repeated a joke that included the word "nigger." We both froze for a second and then moved forward as if nothing had happened. Loud thoughts screamed inside my skull: Is she allowed to say that? Should I say something? What does it mean if I do or don't say something? Is it okay for me to tell that joke but not for her?

I remember thinking, "Am I a race traitor?"

Persia and Me: A Long-Distance Love Affair

I have never been to Iran, and I speak Farsi only on the rare occasions when I am around other speakers. Yet ask me for a list of Persian accomplishments and I will reel off facts from the Achaemenid dynasty through modern-day Iran. I store this information in some mental cabinet, where it is readily accessible and itching to come out. I am proud of being Persian.

If you ask me, however, what Teheran is like at rush hour, or where poets find sanctuary in Shiraz, or what colors can be seen when dusk settles over Abadan's desert terrain, I cannot tell you. I do not know the names of the streets in any Iranian city, which flowers grow in Iran's parks, or the difference between kebab stalls for tourists and those for locals. I have no intimate knowledge of Iranian politics; what I know, I get from the BBC, CNN, and Al Jazeera, just like other Westerners. We Iranians do not have a secret handshake or sly wink to let one another know what's up. I am woefully ignorant of my mother's culture.

That said, when I hear Farsi, I feel like I am home. It is the language I spoke before I learned English. My grandmother and I still speak it together. Its rhythm makes me comfortable, and its melody reminds me of a place to which I am—if only from a long, long distance—connected. My connection to Iran, and my "Iranian-ness," come only from my family and their memories. As they get older, they embellish some moments and downplay others, reworking history into a narrative worth telling. Over time, their stories have become mine; my Iranian identity is a whirlpool of fact, myth, and imagination.

Shaken *and* Stirred

I hate it when people refer to me as half black or half Iranian. I am not half of anything: I am fully black and fully Iranian. Moreover, my identity cannot be reduced to mere fractions. It's complicated but also simple: I am mixed, and there is no personal distress in my being so. Others, however, seem to be confused about my identity.

When I went grocery shopping with my maternal grandmother as a child, people would stare at us and wonder why a black kid was speaking a strange language with an elderly immigrant woman. When I went shopping with my mom, people would congratulate and admire her for adopting a poor colored child. Today, when I go shopping by myself, I occasionally catch people shooting me nervous glances, perhaps thinking I am a thief or a hoodlum or even a terrorist. It appears that I am still somewhat out of place.

"Black American" is a term already fraught with difficulties. For centuries, being black in America was the antithesis of the white American Dream. Being black continues to be associated with aggressiveness, criminality, stupidity, and undesirability. Despite great advances in civil rights, a host of black superstars, and a black president, there is still an outsider status that comes with being black in America.

Being Iranian American does not lessen my personal outsider status. The popular imagination in the West portrays the United States as the vanguard and protector of liberty and democracy, a stalwart ally of the Iranian people, and a beacon of hope in a dark, twisted world. Iranians, so the story goes, have responded to U.S. benevolence with prickly foreign policy, continual criticism, and an unrelenting sense of superiority. The sad reality is that American meddling helped spur (but did not cause) two Iranian revolutions that put the wrong people in power. Put simply, Iranians and Americans have a long-standing beef, and Iranian Americans desperately straddle the fence between their two cultures.

I have often joked with friends that I am America's worst nightmare, as I am both black and Middle Eastern. There is a sad truth in the joke—blacks and Middle Easterners are certainly stereotyped and often portrayed as elements to be feared by much of American society—but also a liberating reality. I never wanted to be the guy who held a corporate job so he could buy the house with the white picket fence, move in with the girl next door, and have 2.5 kids. Growing up, I instinctively knew that that dream was for people who did not look like me, and I did not care. I was left free to explore ways of being that were not scripted on sitcoms and glorified in TV ads. I was not resentful precisely because I did not see my world as "us" versus "them." Instead I saw multiple cultural practices in my home every day; I saw them clash and create new norms; and I saw those norms turn into a culture in and of itself. I saw that nothing was stagnant or fixed or solitary. I saw that I had options.

I was eager to explore the identity choices I found laid before me. Scholars and analysts often talk of "negotiating" or "navigating" identity. Clothing, speech patterns, hairstyles, rebelliousness, athleticism, flirtatiousness—all are used to project identity. Everyone navigates identity, but when race is introduced into the mix, the stakes are raised.

At an early age I learned how to twist my self-presentation to provoke specific responses from those around me. I was eager to figure out what identity I could drape around my shoulders most naturally. It was not the most fun or ho-hum moments that taught me which parts of myself to camouflage or accentuate—quite the opposite. To put it bluntly, I hated being followed around by store security and watching suburbanites cross the street when they saw me approaching. I learned quickly how to use my particular social constructions to my advantage.

I used my mixed identity to convey both positive and negative racial images. For example, I love coffee shops, and grabbing a cup of "joe" is a daily ritual. I choose what I wear each day largely on the basis of how I want to be treated at the coffee shop. If I want to get in and out without any hassles, I wear a black hoodie, basketball sneakers, and worn-out jeans. If I am open to conversing with retired older men sipping their lattes, I wear slacks, a thin sweater, and a trimmed beard. If I want to get some work done, I wear a T-shirt, my good jeans, and a pair of Converse kicks. Here is the fun bit: after I've worn a sweater in order to befriend latte-sipping regulars, when I walk in the next day wearing track pants and a Yankees cap, they often do not recognize me.

During my freshman year of college, I made the mistake of thinking that all liberal arts schools were bastions of liberalism. I dove headlong into a political conversation with a fifty-something academic, assuming he was the sort of person who would appreciate different people's perspectives and backgrounds. He soon started railing, however, about then-candidate Barack Obama and his racial "double bind." According to this gentleman, Obama had either to choose to be black or to claim his mother's whiteness. He could not do both because…well, I'm still unclear about the "why" of it all. I clearly recall the last few moments of our conversation.

| The Gentleman: | "I can tell that you're just going to dismiss what I'm saying because I'm an old white guy." |
| Me: | "No, I'm going to dismiss it because you just don't get it." |

And he didn't. He could not wrap his head around how President Obama's narrative was possible. He was looking right at me, and he could not see a damn thing. I took it personally.

When it comes to issues of race and identity, I am just as confused as everybody else. I speak of social constructs, performances of race, and fluid identities as if they were terms I instinctively understand. The truth is, I spend an obscene amount of time trying to connect clichéd questions like "Where are you from?" and "What makes you who you are?" to abstract conceptions of race, ethnicity, and nationality. I feel immense discomfort sketching even the vaguest outline of myself, as I fear I will exaggerate one part at the expense of another. I fear that I have somehow invested in stereotypical identity narratives that strangle racial discourse, and that I will one day regret typecasting myself within such boundaries.

Most of all, I fear that someone, somewhere, will attempt to extract a morsel of wisdom from my experiences. I do not write this with any intention of being self-deprecating or to downplay the value of my testimony. There is nothing stronger than a voice declaring "I am." It is just that my voice has not yet found its pitch. My questions about identity can be answered with academic theories and clever argumentation, but gut emotion and intellectual satisfaction are distant, distant cousins. In seeking resolution on my "true" identity, I have unstitched and re-sewn pieces of myself more times than I care to count.

Ten years from now, I may fume while reading this account of my life experiences. I may want to take red ink to the page with the fury of a moody English professor. I may think that my twenty-three-year-old self's musings are childish or presumptuous...I don't know. The point is this: I am a work in progress.

After graduating from Dartmouth College, Anise received a Master's of Philosophy in Geography from Queen's University Belfast. He is currently pursuing an MFA in creative writing at Rutgers University (Camden).

11

Dean O'Brien   We Aren't That Different

"*Ni e le ma?*" I ask my grandma. "Are you hungry?" She doesn't respond. She can't hear that well anymore. I ask again. She looks up from her knitting and shakes her head no. She isn't hungry. My mom stepped out to get some groceries and has left me to keep an eye on my grandma. Her health hasn't been the best of late, but she's in all-right shape for her age.

She goes back to her knitting, and after a few minutes she asks me, without looking up, "*Ni juede Beijing hao haishi Shanghai hao?*" I've just gotten back from studying in China, and she wants to know what I thought about the home country.

"*Wo juede suoyou de chengshi hen hao. Danshi dui wo lai shuo Shanghai bi Beijing xiandai.*" (I think all the cities are nice, but in my opinion Shanghai is more modern than Beijing.) I'm struck by the fact that this is the most complicated idea I've expressed to my grandma in my entire life.

She nods and says, "*Wo xiao shihou, wo fuqin dai wo qu Shanghai.*" (When I was little, my father took me to Shanghai.)

We were speaking in Mandarin, a Chinese dialect that neither of us speaks natively. In this conversation I learned more about my grandmother than I had in the first twenty-one years of my life. Speaking slowly, I asked my grandmother about her childhood and her life in China. I learned that my grandma grew up in Fujian Province, a coastal region in southern China. There she spoke the local dialect at home but learned Mandarin in school. She and her family left for Vietnam during the Japanese occupation in World War II, and it was there that she married my grandfather, raised my mother and her other children, and learned Cantonese, the Chinese dialect that my mom's family speaks.

When I was little, I was also able to speak Cantonese, but once I entered school, I pretty much lost it all. My dad can't speak Cantonese, so we didn't speak it at home, and as my English got better and better, my Cantonese fell by the wayside. I can still understand the language, but when it comes to constructing sentences, I'm unable to express even simple ideas.

Before studying Mandarin, the time I spent with my grandma was always awkward. Neither of us could speak the other's language very well, so conversations revolved around yes-or-no questions asked by my grandma, which I did my best to respond to. Once, when I was seventeen, I had to take my grandma on a ninety-minute drive with only the two of us in the car. She tried to make conversation, but whenever she asked me something complicated, I had to respond in Cantonese, "*Ngor m sick gong.*" (I don't know how to say it.) After this happened a few times, she laughed and said to me jokingly, "*Gam do zung man saai saai.*" (So much Chinese wasted.) We were silent again for a little while before she told me that her biggest regret was never learning English.

I sometimes wonder what my grandma thinks of her life in the United States. She's been in this country for over twenty years, but her interactions in that time have been limited to family members and a few Chinese speakers on the occasional trip to Chinatown. I wonder what she thinks of her half-Asian grandchildren who, like me, can't talk with her because we didn't grow up speaking Cantonese with both of our parents.

In our first real conversation after I returned from Beijing, my grandma asked if I had a girlfriend. I said that I did and she asked if she was Chinese. I told her she wasn't. My grandma then jokingly asked, "*Weishenme? Ni bu xihuan zhongguoren ma?*" (Why? You don't like Chinese people?) I didn't have a good answer, but she eased the awkwardness by saying that I should bring my girlfriend to visit sometime.

I probably didn't have an answer for her because I don't often think about race. I know that my mixed racial heritage has colored my experiences in many ways, but not in a way that is exclusive to race. Because I have grown up with two different cultures, the idea that there are multiple valid perspectives on life has always been salient. Therefore, my story isn't really about race but rather about seeing things from different perspectives and, I like to think, being a better person because of it.

Early Days

I grew up in Pleasant Valley, New Jersey, a town that has the same juxtaposition of cultures and values as my family. It is a peculiar mix of new and old and is filled with minor memorials to the past. My elementary school is named after a tavern where General Washington and his soldiers stayed during the American Revolution. The fenced area outside the church on Main Street was used by the Revolutionary army to train and exercise horses. An old schoolhouse, no longer in use, stands on the corner of a now busy road, a testament to the passage of time. Pleasant Valley was once a farming community, and we still have relics from that time as well. Every autumn the town celebrates the Harvest Fair, and Thomas Orchards has its Apple Day. The farming families have mostly gotten out of the business and sold their land, but a few remain. The farming done now is more emblematic than sustaining, but there is a variety of local produce available. The Smith family still runs its corn stand every summer, and a cooperative organic farm allows residents to buy a share of the weekly crops. But this is a different kind of farming, representative of a different kind of people. The blue-collar farmers who once populated our town have been pushed to the periphery by a younger generation interested in products that are organic, fair trade, and carbon neutral.

The farmland has slowly disappeared as neighborhoods have expanded. I grew up in a one-story ranch-style house on the busy main road that runs though Pleasant Valley. For the better part of a decade, I waited outside the house every morning for the bus to take me to school. The bus would pull up and I'd climb on, say hello to Ed, the bus driver, and take my pick of seats; mine was the first stop, so I could sit anywhere on the empty bus. I usually took the seat right behind Ed. He had hair down to his butt, always wore tie-dye, and loved the Grateful Dead. I didn't know anything about the Grateful Dead and didn't understand the mix of skeletons and colorful bears that decorated the bus, but Ed was always interesting to talk to. He was a strange guy, and I think that's why I liked talking to him so much—I felt we both were kind of misfits. Unlike most adults, he was approachable and warm and seemed genuinely interested in whatever opinions my first-grade self cared to share.

Every morning the bus took the slight left onto Jacob's Creek Road and followed the meandering path to Pleasant Ridge, the neighborhood where most of the kids on our route lived. The homes there could only loosely be called houses; "manor" or perhaps "estate" would be more accurate. Each house had a professionally manicured lawn, stately entrance, luxury cars in the driveway, and an immaculate pool in the back. Looking out that bus window, I saw a world that was not my own, and for many years I was envious of the pristine storybook setting that many of my classmates seemed to take for granted.

One of my earliest school friends lived in that neighborhood. Carl had just moved to Pleasant Ridge in the summer before first grade, and we were in the same class. Spending so much time together on the bus and in school, we became fast friends. It was about this time that I began to notice that my family operated very differently from those of my friends. When I visited Carl's home, the first thing I noticed was how clean everything was; his family had a professional housekeeper who came every week to help tidy things up. I didn't know that such things existed. At home, my mom took care of cleaning, and we didn't have the same emphasis on neatness. It's not as if there were dirty dishes everywhere, but things didn't need to be put away if they were going to be used again soon. As long as things were functional, it was fine.

Tony, my closest friend at the time, also lived in a stately home. Both his parents worked in the city, so he was often left in the care of an au pair. This concept was very strange to me. I couldn't understand why parents would want a stranger to live with their family and take care of their children.

Those early experiences with my classmates shaped the way I viewed the world. When I think back on that part of my life, I see that all the social anxieties I felt were a result of the underlying class divide. I felt different from my friends, but it had nothing to do with my race. From a very young age I saw the world as having lots of little self-contained parts. The rich lived a different lifestyle from the rest of us, and when the two worlds interacted, I always felt some discomfort. As I've gotten older, that strict separation of people has seemed to fade. This might be the result of attending a prestigious university and being somewhat more accepted as a member of the elite, but I'd like to think that it stems more from a realization that material differences are superficial. I think I realized this as a child without being able to articulate it.

Still, for the young me, life was made up of little arenas, each of which had its own set of rules, customs, behaviors, and participants. There was a distinct separation between the two large arenas of my childhood: school and hockey. One of my fondest early memories is of sitting in the warm-up room at the old rink at Princeton Day School. Every Saturday in winter my mom would get me up before sunrise, and my dad would take me down to the rink. That rink was the epitome of old-time hockey. It had a roof but was open to the winter elements on three sides. The warm-up room had a little black woodstove with a big pile of logs stacked next to it. As our parents laced up our skates, the only sound we'd hear was the dull roar of the Zamboni resurfacing the ice. When the Zamboni was finished, we'd step out into the foggy rink and skate for the rest of the morning.

Hockey was one place where the ordinary structure of my life was removed. Sure, we had a schedule and the game had rules, but there was never any pressure, and I think that's why I loved it. It didn't matter whether I played well or lost the game for the team. The freedom I had playing hockey was also very different from the structure in my education. The difference in these two parts of my life seemed to represent the differences between my parents.

My dad never pushed me in anything, but when I did show interest in something, he would help me pursue it. At Back to School Night in my junior year of high school, my composition teacher gave the parents a questionnaire to help get to know them and us better. One of the questions was "What are your hopes and dreams for your child?" My teacher showed me what my father wrote: "I have no hopes and dreams for Dean. I only hope that he follows his own." This perfectly captures my father's attitude toward parenting. On weekends, my dad and I often went to coffee shops to sit and read, and to get out of the house. The best part of these outings was the drive over, when we'd talk about everything and anything. I'd often ask my dad for his opinion on the trivial problems I'd been having at school, and he'd give me the same reassuring answer, that I was just stressing over things that didn't matter. We'd talk about the experiments he was running at work and about the new inventions we'd read or heard about. Being with my dad always gave me a release valve; he was a person with whom I could vent my frustrations and who would always listen without condescension. He rarely pressured me, yet I was always aware of what he thought was best.

I had a very different relationship with my mother. She rarely gives praise. Whenever I came home with a grade that was less than perfect, she focused on what I did incorrectly and needed to fix. I hated this and dreaded having to show my mom my tests. When I did get a perfect score, she'd glance at the paper and say, "Okay." Never "Good job." My mother set very high goals for me, and throughout elementary school she would assign me extra work after I finished my homework each day. We fought about it often. I'd tell her that none of my friends had to do extra work. "I don't care what your friends do," she would say, and I'd resign myself to her demands.

My parents argued regularly about how to raise their children. My dad saw my mom's constant pushing of my brother and me as abusive, while my mom saw my dad's laissez-faire attitude as neglectful. Neither could accept the way the other felt because neither could articulate what he or she was trying to do in a way the other could understand. They couldn't see that they both wanted the same thing: to give their kids the skills we needed to survive on our own. I can see now that neither my dad's loose attitude nor my mom's rigid structure alone would have been very good for me. Without my mom pushing, I wouldn't have a strong educational foundation, but without my dad, I would have lost the desire to learn a long time ago.

My mother and father can see the world only from their own perspectives, but now that I'm out of the house and my brother will be soon, my parents don't fight like they used to. They don't argue, but I wouldn't say things are better between them. They don't sleep in the same room anymore, the house I grew up in is falling apart, and they both seem unhappy, yet neither can manage to leave. Maybe deep down they really don't want to, or maybe they're too broken/dependent/loving/fearful to break it off and start over. I think my parents were never really able to see beyond their cultural differences.

For many years my parents argued about my mother's mismanagement of her medication. She has bipolar disorder, and when I was a kid, she was in and out of psychiatric facilities because of her inability to stay on her medication. My father couldn't understand why it was so difficult for her to take a pill every morning, but more critically, he could not understand how strong the stigma of mental illness is in Chinese society. When I was younger, I couldn't really understand it either. I couldn't understand why my mom would continually take herself off the medication she so clearly needed.

I was in second grade when my mom was first hospitalized. For several days her behavior became less and less like that of the mom I had known. The living room floor was covered with pages of ink sketches, each one slightly different but done with the same hurried hand. Chinese and French songs echoed eerily through the hallways. The mom I knew didn't draw. She also never sang. My mom's family didn't make things any easier. They couldn't accept that my mother's illness was the result of a chemical imbalance and thus they blamed my father, saying he was the one who made her crazy.

I didn't understand why my mom found it difficult to stay on her medication until I was faced with a similar experience in my own life. During my sophomore year of high school I was diagnosed with juvenile rheumatoid arthritis. For six months, doctors tried to get my immune system under control, and they eventually found a medication that worked. The medication had to be injected, and they said I would have to take it every week for the rest of my life. This idea didn't sit well with me. I couldn't accept that I would have to take medication forever in order to have a normal life. So I took myself off it. At that moment I truly understood why it would be difficult for my mom to accept that she had to take a pill every morning for the rest of her life, even though it clearly helped her stay "sane."

I guess it comes down to being able to empathize with others. Often the only way to do that is to have walked in another's shoes and experienced life the way that person does. In a cultural and racial sense, I grew up living two lives and experiencing two cultures. I'm most grateful for this aspect of my upbringing.

Later Days

At my maternal grandmother's house, conversations were always infused with collectivist values. My grandma and aunts would tell me to keep an eye out for my younger brother. In their eyes, if he did anything wrong, it was partly my fault. This held true for all of us. If I did something wrong, it was partially my cousins' fault because they should have been keeping track of me. There was never any distinction between siblings and cousins; all the kids were lumped together. We spent more time with extended family than most kids I knew. When I was little, I asked my mom why we did this, but she didn't seem to understand the question. To her, family is the most important thing, so spending so much time at Grandma's was what we should do. I don't want to imply that I disliked our family time; I actually enjoyed it and think I'm closer to my aunts, uncles, and cousins than most other people are to theirs.

My family experience was certainly different from what I experienced at school, where there was always an emphasis on self-sufficiency and an underlying belief that you alone own your successes and failures. My teachers told my parents that I was a quick learner, which was probably due more to the extra homework I did with my mom than to any individual quality I possessed. I think there are advantages and disadvantages to experiencing different worldviews. I've tried to experience life from as many angles as I can in the hope that I'll never get stuck believing or doing something that doesn't make me happy.

I've tried to stay friends with a wide variety of people, and my best friends are some of the strangest people I know. For four years I played on my high school ice hockey team, which was full of clowns. Of all the athletes in the school, the hockey team had the lowest GPA. We were the only team that had mandatory afterschool study halls because some play-ers were in danger of becoming academically ineligible for sports. These guys couldn't take anything seriously, but I couldn't have asked for better teammates. Playing on that team helped me keep everything in perspec-tive and reminded me that not everything in life should be serious.

I had a lot of friends in high school who were really into live music, psychedelic art, hiking, and the environment—a kid from suburban New Jersey's version of the counterculture. There's a nature preserve at the edge of our town that has miles of trails cut through it. My friends and I spent countless days hiking through this area. This was our sanctuary, a piece of the world that was entirely our own. A long time ago, glaciers carved the terrain of the preserve and left behind huge rock formations. We nicknamed one of them the Hippie Rock. We'd bring beer and maybe some pot, and spend endless summer days there lounging on the rocks, hidden by the surrounding forest. We'd talk about anything—music, phi-losophy, girls, sports. It was our oasis from the real world where we could simply be carefree. It was a welcome contrast to the pressures that came with high school, college admissions, and growing up.

My hometown is a mostly white, liberal area, and because of this, most of my friends were white and pretty liberal. In high school, when we dis-cussed national issues, the conservative argument was often ridiculed, which is the background I brought with me to college. I have to say that I'm happy to have had the privilege of meeting so many people there whose beliefs are different from my own.

When I first arrived at college, the presidential primaries had just begun. Since our school is in New Hampshire, which has the first primary, it was a big deal. It was in this environment that I had my first real experi-ence with conservatism. While drinking beers together, some of my floor mates and I discussed how we felt about the candidates and the direction of our country. I don't really remember who said what, but I do remember being asked questions that I'd never expected from conservatives. These were rational people with rational concerns, and they were asking the same kinds of questions my liberal friends would ask. For the first time the con-servative position made sense to me, and I liked that. These people were very different from the gay-bashing Bible thumpers who used to come to mind when I heard the word "conservative." As with my parents and their beliefs on parenting, the differences I saw between conservatives and liberals were differences in application. The goal for both groups was the same: a better country.

At college I got another opportunity to branch out in a way that I couldn't in my hometown. College was the first place I'd been that had a number of Asian Americans, and by extension a fair number of Asian and Asian American organizations. I'd never been in any predominantly Asian groups before, so I went to the meetings of a couple of these organizations. After a few meetings, though, I decided they weren't for me. I didn't fit in, I didn't speak any Asian language well, and I just felt that I didn't have much in common with the people in these groups. I didn't have many Asian friends while growing up, and it struck me that most of these people hung out almost exclusively with other Asians. I guess when I went to the meetings, I felt like I was faking something. As a half-Asian kid, I felt as if people at these meetings expected me to be someone that I wasn't; there was an implicit pressure to like everything about Asian culture simply because it was our heritage. I just wasn't into any of it as much as everyone else seemed to be. I was just looking for a place to hang out with people who had a similar cultural background. I stopped going to the meetings.

Nevertheless, during my sophomore year I found I did want some connection with my Asian heritage. I hadn't yet fulfilled the language requirement for graduation, so I decided to take Chinese. After completing first-year Chinese, I had to choose whether to continue with my Chinese studies. I decided that I didn't want all the work I had done to go to waste, so I went on the foreign study program to Beijing.

I was excited about going to China for two main reasons. Before going to China, I'd never left the East Coast. I guess I'm pretty homegrown, and since all our family lives in the Northeast, I'd never gone anywhere else. So I was excited about going to China simply to visit someplace different. More important, though, I was excited about getting in touch with a part of my background in a way that I never had been able to do on my own. Whenever we went to Chinatown, I had relied on a family member to communicate. By going to Beijing, I'd be able to experience China and explore my Chinese-ness on my own. Before studying Chinese, I was afraid that as I got older, I'd be locked out of lots of the things I did as a kid because my language skills weren't very good, such as going to the markets or restaurants in Chinatown. It was mostly this fear that pushed me to continue my Chinese studies.

A few months before going to China, I was with my aunt at Jin Men, a grocery store near her house that sells Chinese food. I could read a few characters on the labels of the items for sale, and I heard phrases that were straight out of the dialogues we had meticulously memorized for class. "*Wo zai nar fu qian?*" (Where do I pay?). "*Yigong shi duo shao qian?*" (What's the total?). For the first time these foreign sounds made sense to me outside the sterile academic environment of the classroom. This was real life, where real people were going about their daily lives.

On my first day in China, I was up at 5:00 a.m. because of jet lag, so I decided to go out and get breakfast on my own. I found stands all around selling dumplings called *baozi;* each serving plate has anywhere from eight to twelve, depending on where you buy them. I wanted only half an order, but I didn't know what the measure word was. Should I say a plate? A serving? A tray? I went up to the *fuwuyuan,* the service person, and asked for *yi ban* (one-half). She looked at me confused and asked, *"Yi pan?"* (One tray?).

"Bu shi. Wo zhi yao yi ban." (No, I just want a half).

She was still confused, so I told her that I wanted six *baozi.*

"Liu fen baozi?" (Six orders of dumplings?).

I still couldn't get my meaning across, and ended up just motioning that I only wanted half the tray. She finally understood. It was frustrating, but I chalked that one up in the win column because I ended up with what I wanted.

On one of the first days we were in Beijing, my friend Peter and I were exercising at the university's track. All around the city and the university campus we had seen proclamations on large banners that promoted the Chinese nation or the Communist Party. At the track we saw a similar banner and wondered what it meant. "Hmm, 'Every day [two unintelligible Chinese characters] an hour,'" I said. "I wonder what that means." "I don't know either," Peter replied, and we forgot about it. A few days before we left Beijing, we were back at the track and noticed the same banner. We turned to each other and laughed because sometime during the last three months we had learned the missing characters. It read "Exercise one hour every day."

Before going abroad, I had been pretty convinced that learning a new language was simply beyond my ability. But once I was there, more and more of the world around me became accessible as I learned more and more of the language. It wasn't easy, and at times it was pretty frustrating, but being in China was one of the most rewarding experiences of my life.

There were things I had expected to be very different in China that ended up being similar to how they are in the States. For example, in one of our classes we got to see a documentary about the indie rock scene in China. There were punk rockers with Mohawks and tattoos, and teenagers with shaggy hair and skinny jeans—things that I didn't expect to see in China. I guess I expected China to have one culture, as if all the Chinese would believe and act the same way. I expected everyone to be really excited about Spring Festival or making dumplings or something like that. It wasn't rational, but it was the image I had in the back of my mind. I also hadn't expected the regional differences we encountered in both language and customs. In Beijing, for example, you call waitresses *fuyuyuan*, but in other parts of the country you call them *xiaojie*, a form of address which is considered offensive in Beijing.

After being in China I started to feel that for the most part everyone everywhere is fundamentally the same. China is a communist country; a council appoints the president. The government screens movies and television to look for political criticism. Even Facebook and YouTube are blocked. And yet people's lives are more or less the same as they are in the United States. Shopkeepers run their shops, office workers go to work, professors teach, students learn, and life goes on. Sure, the faces are different, the food's a little unfamiliar, and everything has Chinese characters on it, but these are just surface differences. I think I feel that way about being biracial. There are clear and undeniable differences between the Asian and Caucasian sides of my family, but on a more fundamental level they are exactly the same. Both my mom and my dad and all my aunts, uncles, cousins, and grandparents care for me; they just show it in different ways. Every country, every ethnicity, and every family has its own different set of values, traditions, and customs. When it comes right down to it, you just have to find what's right for you.

As for me, I've discovered that I'm not Chinese and I'm not Caucasian. There are customs that I like and values that are important to me from each, but I'm not simply a sum of these two parts. To describe my racial heritage is simply that—a description of one aspect of my life. There's a lot more to the story, and I can't talk about my life without talking about all the other parts—my friends, my hometown, or the meandering experiences that have shaped the way I view the world—because all of them are an equal part of who I am.

After graduating from college, Dean moved to New York City to work as a consultant. He plans to return to academia to pursue a Ph.D. in computational neuroscience.

12

Lola Shannon Finding Zion

I have never lived in a household with both my parents. The most obvious part of their relationship was that they were apart...far apart. My mother raised me by herself. Even when given the chance to care for me during visits, my father never struck me as a parent. To my mind, his presence during my childhood was blurred into a general sense of mystique about his position in our lives. There was a large contrast between everyday life with my mother and the times I spent with my father, when elegant meals out and shopping sprees at his expense were the norm. When I was small, however, I couldn't see that he was leading a comparably privileged life, and that being without him added to my mother's financial struggle.

My maturation and the progression of poverty in my home eventually caused me to resent my father's lack of support. A few years before he died, a complex war began between me and my father that shaped my adolescence. This was very different from the friction I experienced with my mother. We were close, sometimes too close to work out our problems, while my father was a mythical and, at best, a magical figure. He was capable of appearing and transforming parts of my life (at least by providing material souvenirs of our relationship and puzzling words of wisdom) and then disappearing for extended periods of time. This fluctuation made me feel only half visible, so that by the age of thirteen, I had pretty much given up on getting to know him.

Sometimes I felt pushed and pulled by my mother, too. Because of our closeness—to the point of sharing dreams and telepathy—my mother's problems often spilled over onto me. It is important to say that through all the bad times, what has kept us, and will keep us, able to understand each other deeply is my mother's persistence in a world of obstacles. Ingenuity with scarce resources and taking pride in my voice are things I learned from my mother. A key part of her determination to be herself was refusing to depend on a man in any way. Another part was working hard to accommodate her desire to be a writer. But my mother also struggles with the scars of mistreatment stemming from times far before she had me. Ironically, the strength I admired often put a strain on our household. She was a practicing alcoholic until I was eight years old. Although I am thankful that she drank only when I was in bed at night, I do remember terrifying experiences like not being able to wake my mum at noon on weekends.

For the most part, the earlier years of my life passed by with ease. I remember living with my mum and my grandmother, whom we call Pedey, in a tiny apartment when I was three. I knew that Pedey thought I was special, and I loved her very much. My mum moved in with Pedey because she was having financial problems. My dad had left her pregnant in Toronto, forcing her to move back east to New Brunswick. When my dad left to return to Jamaica, every month for a year he promised he'd be back and then we would all live together again. During the next seventeen years, he never came to Canada for more than a week. My cousin Sophie also lived in the same city. We were like sisters since I was born only three months after her. We used to take off our clothes and dance for an admiring audience of three: her mum, my mum, and Pedey. There I was, a little brown body, dancing among all the white bodies. I never imagined I was different.

When I was three, Mum and I went to Jamaica to visit my dad. We had been once before when I was one, but what I mostly remember from that trip is more the feeling of Jamaica than my father. I remember sitting in the backseat of the car, my eyes softened to the somehow familiar air. I saw the white face of my mother and the dark brown face of my father side by side. They were smiling as my mother fed me little bits of spicy Jamaican patties. I remember slowly grasping the little pieces and enjoying them both for their taste and for the way in which my mum carefully handled them. My eyes watered from the spice, and I reached for more. The sound of my mother and father laughing together made the car seem an insufficient container for our happiness.

My second trip to Jamaica at three years old was quite different. I really recognized my dad. The smell of sugar cane in the heat and the black leather of his car were signals for me of his identity. But these elements didn't make me feel very much a part of this man. I still didn't see him as my father. I was living in a temperate world where fatherhood was defined by bedtime stories and next-door neighbors. My mum reminds me of periods of time I would spend, when I could just barely speak, saying over and over "Ted?…Ted? Dad, Ted?" My pronunciation was not so precise, but she would desperately explain that, no, my daddy was not dead but in Jamaica, and she would take me to the map and show me where it was.

For a long time my father would retain a tenuous connection to a part of me which was hard to articulate. This connection was not yet a negative thing. My mum encouraged me to accept my Jamaican as well as my Canadian blood. Some days she would set me up finger painting to reggae, other days to Beethoven. As I grew from toddler to child, I'm sure I tasted the soil of another land on my tongue and I perspired the salt water of the "likkle rock" when I ran. These sensations were home to me, as were wintry air on my cheek, and dandelions. But because they were so familiar, I didn't differentiate between the two. My world as a child was comfortable, home-oriented, and private. I could play out the extent of either culture without interference. What triggered the sense of separation was the awareness and comprehension that my father was not around.

Starting school was for me the entrance into a period of malaise about my home life. I used to print "I don't have one" on personal information forms for school when asked about my father's name or occupation. I figured that a daddy must be something like a dog. I didn't have one, and whether it got hit by a car or ran away didn't matter because it happened before I was born. Friends started asking me where he was from. "Jamaica," I replied. I could point it out on the map for them. I didn't get offended when they asked if it was like Hawaii.

One girl at school used to think it was just the best joke to ask me, "Are you black or did you just take a bath in really dirty water?" I was honestly perplexed by this at first, thinking how could dirt be compared with having darker-than-white skin? Then it hit me that each time kids looked at me, they saw my difference as negative. When a girl befriended me, I began to feel that it was only because she felt pity for me. When the boys locked me in their playhouse or pushed me off the swing, I felt that they were trying somehow to modify me. I began to feel too exposed. I didn't like to be where everybody could see me.

I got into biking everywhere, so that no one could look at me for a very long time. I would even have my mother stuff my bicycle into the trunk of her car each day so I could bike around at lunch and to after-school care. I was beginning to be embarrassed by my faraway father because he represented a large part of why I didn't fit in where I lived, and he wasn't even around to help me with it. There were numerous times when my parents would talk about living together again, which would make me ecstatic. Not only would I be part of a "normal" family, but also I would have some clout behind my skin color. My community would recognize us as a unit and be less likely to mess with me.

There were limits to how much my mother could help me deal with racism as a child. Primarily this was because I hadn't yet learned concepts like discrimination. But another reason was my sense that my mum had never had to endure what was making me feel so out of sorts. I was around four years old when I began to notice the differences between Mum and me. She didn't have as much trouble as I did combing her hair in the morning. One day in the sun would turn me a deep brown, whereas she would redden. And there were other things I couldn't quite pinpoint until I was older. She seemed very much at ease with other people, and would often invite women over for tea. An acquired mistrust of white people caused me to skulk in corners during these visits. My mum would have to urge me to "come and say 'Hi,' Lola."

I changed schools in second grade because I was so unhappy. In my new school I finally found a group of real friends. But gradually, throughout elementary school, they lost interest in me as they learned what was "cool" and what was not. To deal with the cues that I was not quite right, I gravitated toward the other outcasts: an Indian girl who bought me a bag of chips every day to guarantee my companionship, an Egyptian boy, a Jewish boy, and a girl with a learning disability. I did get on the good side of one "regular" girl, however. Her name was Penny. She was tormented by boys because of her daring nature. She was small and fast enough to carry out any stunt she could dream up. I admired Penny and took the chance with her to express my naturally outgoing personality. We were the leaders in kissing tag or Chinese skipping, and we managed to be the loudest girls without being considered "conceited" in the judgmental eyes of the other school kids. We were among the few girls who could adeptly play rebound with the boys—no matter how hard the ball was whipped at the brick building.

The only thing was, Penny was pretty and I wasn't. She had straight, fine hair, and when all the boys called her "fountain head," I knew it was a compliment. She was shorter than the guys, so they took her seriously when she asked them to the dance. Whenever I "asked out" a boy, he would answer, "Why would I go out with you, you're just another boy. You play with the boys, you have short hair—it would be like me going out with Jeff. Hey, Jeff, come here! Will you go out with me, Jeff?" I tried to blend in by adding to the laughter, but every comment like that took chunks out of my ego. These white guys were telling me that I had no beauty. If I had beauty, it wasn't decipherable to them, and therefore I wasn't recognizable as a female. I was generally seen as a tomboy.

At that point I would have given anything for a friend who cherished me as much as I did her. I began to spend more time with my best friend, Jan, whom I had met when I was six. I was devoted to her for years. I didn't branch out at all in junior high. I wasn't provided with very many opportunities to make new friends. I certainly couldn't fit into any of the many cliques that formed at my new school. The kids would gather in the parking lot at lunch hour, forming tight circles according to who belonged to what group. These groups didn't budge unless someone passing by was recognized as a member and allowed to shuffle in. There was a sense of urgency about their huddle. If I ever tried to talk to anyone in a circle, I was physically elbowed out without a word. No explanation, just rejection. My cousin Sophie, the one I used to dance with, participated in this. Alone she was great. Thinking back, I find it ironic that this experience in the parking lot which I found so shocking was going on inside the building in more subtle ways.

I think in my attempt to mask my insecurities, I probably came across as a confident adolescent. That's how I got through junior high. In class, when I practically whispered, *"J'ai dix ans,"* everybody chimed in with "You're only ten?!" I didn't look like the other girls at all because I couldn't afford their clothes and makeup, and because I didn't know how to make myself appear like the others. They were all white, except the one Indian girl with whom I had been friends in elementary school, but she had given up on talking by this time. In fact, I could count on one hand the number of people in my junior high school who weren't white. Out of nine hundred, there was one Egyptian girl who was very popular and looked white, one well-liked black and one delinquent black, one East Indian, and a handful of Aboriginals.

The alienation was too much to cope with. I began to suffer periods of depression. Probably the one thing, besides Jan, that kept me going was my ability to write, paint, play violin, and dance. My mum encouraged me to work hard at my extracurricular activities because she knew how unhappy I was at school. Thinking it was simply due to boredom, she fought hard to add enrichment to my school life, which is why I ended up skipping the last grade of elementary school. Nonetheless, for half a year I spent many of my school days in the health room with the lights out. I felt like my intestines were being eaten away. When I was in class,

I'd daydream constantly. My marks stayed slightly above average, which I suppose gave the teachers reason not to worry too much about my state. I survived by fantasizing. I'd think about where I would go if I wasn't stuck in New Brunswick, if one of my mum's frequent plans for starting a new life would really occur. What would happen if we actually had enough money to act like a normal family, or even what I'd do if any guy saw me as attractive.

But I was a nerd. And because my sexuality was becoming a stronger and stronger force inside me, it was a particularly terrible time for me to feel disliked. Not one guy took me seriously. I couldn't always connect it consciously with racism, but I often could. I heard a lot of "psss-sss...that nigger" when I walked the halls. One day I was walking home when I heard a shout from above—"Hey, Oreo!"—which was engulfed by laughter as the window slammed shut. I looked around and didn't see any walking cookies, so I continued on. I was enraged when a guy who claimed he was my friend called me a nigger.

"Don't call me a nigger, Jamie. Don't call me that!"
"Nigger! Nigger! Nigger-nigger-nigger." His laughter made me dizzy.
"Don't call me a nigger, JAMIE! Please, don't call me that! "I was almost
   crying by now. "If you call me a nigger, Jamie...I'll kick you in the balls!
   I'll kick you in the balls. I'm not even black, don't you know..."
"Nigger! Nigger! Ha-ha. Nigger!"

He thought it was a game to dodge my swinging book bag and laughed all the way out of the building. He wouldn't stop even when the teacher passed by us numerous times, seemingly oblivious to the savage attack. No matter how often this ritual occurred, I could never bring myself to kick him in the balls. I thought it would be too painful; I could empathize with pain all too easily. Because he was my friend every other minute of the day, I thought my anger and humiliation were irrational. Not only was I dumbfounded by the behavior of my peers, but also I couldn't justify my own feelings.

In grade nine I really wanted to visit my dad again. It had been five years since I'd been to Jamaica, and I was becoming increasingly geared toward that part of my heritage. I was hooked on the reggae albums my dad had sent me when I was little, but I needed to hear living Jamaicans talk to me. As my marginalization in school became unbearable, my instinct was to explore what made me different. I hoped to find sameness, or at least a nicer kind of different. I wanted to be part of a culture so that I had something to defend myself with, a base from which to grow. I feared losing my authenticity if I didn't know anything about Jamaica.

My father didn't spend very much time with me when I arrived in Jamaica, because, as usual, he was working frantically on a project, so I hastily took advantage of alternative welcoming arms. I met two guys on the beach in Ocho Rios, and we arranged to meet later. We walked through the streets of the city and talked into the night. The flood of attention unglued my strong grip on my behavior. In fact, I initiated sneaking onto the beach. I abruptly hopped up and scaled the fence, ending up suspended on the barbed wire, anxious to get down before the trotting security guard arrived from down the path. Rowan gracefully unhooked me and we decided to call it a night.

Later on that night my boldness grew even greater. "I was aiming for your mouth," I said, when he turned his cheek to my kiss. "Oh! In that case, come over here," he replied. We moved behind a bush for a real kiss. This was my first taste of what would become my drug of choice, sexual affection. As we kissed, I wondered what that hard thing digging into my pelvis was. It must be his belt, I thought.

I literally stumbled back to the hotel room, arriving forty-five minutes before curfew, and feeling satisfied. I felt so female! I slept like a baby and woke up the next morning to find blood on the crotch of my bathing suit. I assumed it was a hormonal reaction to getting my first kiss. I didn't understand that I had gotten my first period until I reached home and Mum explained. I was relieved she didn't slap my cheeks so they would be forever rosy like I'd seen in a foreign film. That trip was very important. I began to see myself as attractive. After all the guys who had yelled out "Cris chile! Can I talk?" how could I feel undesirable anymore? I categorized my beauty, though, as measurable solely in Jamaican terms. Only Jamaican guys stared at me like that. When I arrived back in New Brunswick, nothing much had changed. With a bit more gusto, I shook my braids around in gym class and gave presentations and speeches on Jamaica. Some students did react to me, but they seemed both annoyed and surprised that I dared to insist on a foreign identity.

I was beginning to see my relationship with Jamaica as separate from my relationship with my father. I had a physical, genetic, and psychic connection with this island, and I wanted to consider myself Jamaican. I started listening to reggae a lot more. With every drumbeat and every touch of a guitar string, my soul ached to go back. I was a wailer, just like Bob Marley, whose songs of being separated from his motherland were always on my tongue. I could allow myself to detach from my father when he hadn't written in months, yet to stay in love with a culture that I thought I could count on.

This perspective would become even more useful through my years in high school. I adopted Jamaica as my sexual medallion, relying on my color and appearance to attract guys' attention. I went for the ones I knew I could snag. To Jan and me, the next-best thing to Jamaicans were Africans, and we started seeing two university students from southern Africa. Hardly a weekend went by when we weren't attending some international student function at the university campus.

Johnson was my boyfriend, a skinny, decrepit-looking guy with an apologetic smile. In retrospect, I view the nine months I spent as Johnson's girlfriend as a period of time when I was most openly degraded because of my skin color. At first Jan and I didn't take any of it too seriously. One day at Johnson and Oliver's apartment, as we sat draped over their furniture lazily peeling oranges, Jan rolled her eyes to signal she was bored. I twisted my face in empathy. We stuffed the oranges in our mouths whole and had a fit of muffled hysteria while the two guys looked on in perplexity and eventually left the room. To us, they were regular sex, headaches, and free tickets to meet real men. Jan and I were only putting up with them in hopes of finding more fulfilling relationships. In the end, my position in that community would backfire.

By fifteen, my life seemed to be opening up. I was hanging around a crowd of people who were mature enough to talk to and also had apartments and cars. Being surrounded by so many black people made me delirious. At Caribbean Night, I would become a different person. But sometimes a woman's voice or a hand gesture would make me homesick and I would look at Jan and realize she was still white. If I behaved the right way, I could be at best inconspicuous. It had never occurred to me before that the person I was closest to rarely had to deal with what plagued me daily. To socialize with these people she didn't diminish her differences, as I did. She had a more casual attitude toward it, and was probably drawn to these activities out of a thirst for exoticism. Her friendship, however, and our new pastime were making life exciting for the time being.

After a couple of months my relationship with Johnson was doomed. I couldn't put up with his possessiveness any longer. When Johnson sensed I was losing interest, he did everything he could to gain control. He let loose a temper I had never seen in him before. Even though I risked being cut off from the community I had joined through my relationship with

Johnson, I decided to break up with him. A while later I went to a party on my own, but he was living close by, and when he heard where I was, he tracked me down and chased after me. I pleaded with the host of the party, a guy from Kenya, for some help. I was scared. He told me with a smirk to go hide in the tree outside. Suddenly it hit me that I couldn't count on any of these people. After I found a dark room to lock myself up in, I gave in to the realization that if I wished to have any relationships with these guys, it would be on only a very superficial and unequal basis. I shrank back into the bed as Johnson began to pound ferociously on the door. This time he was threatening to kill me. The wood was cracking, and with the music now turned down, I could hear the splinters land on the linoleum. When he got too disruptive, a group of guys pinned him to the wall, and I escaped home.

From then on I maintained my attachment to that crowd in a less visible way, through almost purely sexual relationships. I wanted to become less of a member of the community by interacting in private. Of course, there is always a system of gossip that makes it hard to maintain privacy in any community. I don't know how much of a part that played in my denigration, but I was "put in my place" in the most effective and harmful way possible.

Immediately after I broke up with Johnson, I was date-raped by a twenty-seven-year old from Saint Lucia. My denial of having been raped, which lasted for weeks, was proof of how dependent I was on the attention and pseudo-acceptance of my little community. I continued to see the guy and acted as though nothing had happened. I didn't even tell Jan or my mum. Even now, after counseling sessions and vivid flashbacks, I can rearrange my "No" and his intimidating coercion into an almost normal scenario. It comforts me like a horror movie with a happy ending. That assault marred my sexuality with a tangle of confusion, remorse, and often unmanageable anger. It was easier to follow a path of unhealthy relationships than to allow the powerful emotions around being violated to bleed into my sex.

Around that time, the scene at school didn't offer many alternatives for socializing. Even more exclusionary than junior high, my new environment offered me one niche: as a member of "the black table" in the cafeteria. We would all gather there at lunchtime to discuss our dance club practices and joke around. When the principal walked by, he would send an unforgiving stare our way as if trying to decipher our next planned action toward the school's demise. We were all supposed to be failures and troublemakers. Unfortunately, some of the black students bought into this stereotype. After so many years of reinforcement from their teachers and friends, they acted out the expected part of the inarticulate jester. I can think of only a few black students who weren't either in dance club or on a sports team, and many took more than three years to graduate. The stereotyped characteristics that allowed them to be a part of the school social system were their energy and loud, humorous way of interacting with people. Some were better than others at behaving this way, and they became the most popular black people around. Although I was perceived to be black in this group, I knew I was different from them. Not just because I was a "café au lait"; I didn't walk the walk or talk the talk very much beyond dancing and laughing. Additionally, I had constant encouragement at home to expand my knowledge and artistic expressiveness. I know I had a better base from which to modify my situation than did the other black students, who came from less-educated, even poorer families.

For example, at one point in grade eleven when I was threatening to leave school, my mother arranged a private course with a Jamaican African man at the local university. By guiding me in my exploration of Caribbean literature, my new mentor taught me how to answer some of the important questions I had about my race. I began to understand why I was often perceived as superior to the darker, full-black Jamaican. Quite a paradox for me to swallow when so often I had been feeling not black enough. The times when Jamaican men ran up to my dad complimenting him on his "beautifully complexioned daughter" now made sense.

My feelings toward Jamaica changed. In light of its sexist, patriarchal organization, my Jamaican identity became less of a mental solace. I was in the middle of defining my feminist beliefs and coping with my anger toward the male culture. Jamaica has such a blatant tradition of degrading women, which is clear in many pieces by its female writers.

The course also triggered a lot of disgust for my father. Since he had never explained himself, I could only assume that his behavior as a father was simply a product of his culture. And how could my mother have been so naïve, I wanted to know. I began to ask her more about the conditions of her relationship with my father. Her responses never satisfied me: it was the seventies, there was a stronger atmosphere of interracial harmony, and they were deeply, deeply in love. Being the living outcome of all this, I was cynical. I felt more independent from my mother because I could understand her less. A violent defiance awoke inside me.

By the time I was in grade twelve, I felt ready to explode—a new emotion for me, as I had generally been in control of my feelings. I had put up with too many abusive relationships, between the racism at school and my unbalanced social life. I was through with feeling like my insides were boiling away; I needed to take care of myself. Without warning, a crisis occurred. I wrote about the experience a little while after it happened: "This morning the grayness of my town rode with me on the school bus up the hill. I thought it was going to be just another day of numbing myself in order not to explode."

I got my books easily; there wasn't much of a locker crunch on a Tuesday morning. I made it easily to my homeroom. I didn't even bother to walk along "Main Street" to see who had made it to school. I knew Jan was probably at home sick again. During the monotonic announcements, I prepared myself for the cold day ahead and then set off for class, excited about getting back a test I thought I had aced.

As the tests were being passed back, people were smiling, so I felt optimistic. When I got my paper back, I stared at my mark—practically a failure. I had studied so much. I could concentrate on only one sentiment: no matter how hard I try to be recognized, commended I never am.

I needed to get out…

From the top of the hill I could see the gray water, and my house seemed miles away. It was the longest walk ever down Fern Street. I wished I could just fall and cry and pull my hair and roll and trip all the way down. When I finally reached home, I fumbled with the screen door in a mess of fresh tears, and Mum greeted me through the glass. She opened the door and extended a wing-like arm. She uttered a phrase of receptivity and hung my coat on a hook. "I'm never going back there…I refuse to go back there." She knew me well enough to realize I meant it.

Dropping out of school seemed arrogant and senseless to many people, but even though she didn't understand all the social turmoil I was experiencing, my mother was always behind me. She sensed that I deeply needed to grant myself a sense of dignity that I had been denied over the years in school. Being expected to shovel in loads of ethnocentric material and to contort myself in a constant effort to be inoffensive had damaged me. The point in my life where I refused to take any more is something I'll always be proud of. I certainly would not be who or where I am today if I had not done it.

At the time, however, it was unrealistic to think about going anywhere without a diploma. I was lucky enough to be invited to spend a term as an auditor at an American college by a family friend. Taking university classes, where the pace was fast and the material intriguing, proved to be highly therapeutic for me. After taking classes in feminism, science, and moral development, I knew more clearly what I wanted to study. My time off allowed me to learn much. I did myself a lot of good, but I also got into bad situations with alcohol and guys. I was still reeling from an emptiness inside me. By standing up for what I needed, I had distanced myself from others. For instance, things were never really the same again with Jan because of our now divergent life goals. When I did return to New Brunswick, to attend a private high school for a year, it was in a different city.

This school was supposed to be geared toward people who needed more academic challenge and who had faced various social problems in public school. I was awarded a half-tuition scholarship, and my father agreed to pay the rest. Once I adjusted to the new environment (I had gone from the largest high school in Canada to the smallest), I was faced with the extreme measures of control imposed on the students' lives.

What I will always refer to as "corruption" was ingrained into this institution and could never be explained in a few lines. My friends and I put up with basic injustices on a daily basis. I did make really close friends, which was the only worthwhile part of that year besides my diploma. We helped one another get by. I stuck it out because I so desperately wanted to get away, out of the Maritimes to study at university.

Then something happened that depleted my psyche so immeasurably that I would be changed forever. I was feeling particularly deserted by my father. When would this sense of desertion end? I wanted to put an end to my foreigner status in my father's world. It was time; I was about to begin taking the steps into an adult lifestyle.

Every step I took on that manicured high school campus reminded me of how I would soon live. I would be so much happier as a university student. At the same time, I was often haunted by images of my mother coming to my classroom to tell me my father was dead. It made each sinew of my body vibrate with tragedy. Any chance of our having a meaningful relationship would be shot. I also think I imagined his death because I resented my dependence on him financially. University would necessitate even greater reliance on him, to which he had agreed, but I didn't like feeding off of someone who was merely an occasional voice on the phone or a signature on a birthday card.

My father had not been in touch since our last visit. As with my other visits to Jamaica during high school, I went with Jan. Normally we had a lot of fun, and my dad's preoccupation with work didn't bother us since we had other things to fill our time with! But in my senior year we spent two mind-boggling weeks on the island. My dad was acting deranged. He would sleep at weird hours and not wake up even when we pounded on his bedroom door. He went to meet people in deserted places and kept thousands of dollars under the mat in his car. He seemed to have lost his appetite and forgotten about ours. He wouldn't take us to eat for days at a time. Since he didn't keep much food in the house, we went hungry. After a few days we became delirious and exhausted. One day we even set out to walk to the nearest town, which was at least twenty-five miles away, to go to the market. We didn't even make it out of his village, and when we returned, we began to panic. But the real conflict started when my dad announced we weren't acting appropriately in front of guys. We demanded to know what he meant. It turned out that our clothes were too revealing, and that basically a woman was responsible for the way men acted toward her! I had never heard such a derogatory comment from my father. I lost it. The rage was consuming. I screamed that he wasn't even around to protect me from all the things guys did to me, he didn't even know what happened. Jan asked him if he thought it was a woman's fault if she was raped. I tore the banister off the new addition to his house and threw some stuff around. Then we told him to take us to Ocho Rios and leave us alone, which he did for a whole week. In the midst of all this Jan and I both caught a tropical disease, and we wound up in the hospital when we finally returned to Canada.

Needless to say, I was not particularly receptive to my father after that visit. He wrote me a letter expressing a desire to form a more compatible relationship, but his tone was so condescending that I crumpled it up. Anyway, it was too late. I was rude about taking money from him and never spoke to him on the phone. The three thousand miles between us complicated communication at the best of times. Now I used it to distance myself from him emotionally. My love for him was interwoven too tightly with pain. I tried to let myself despise him.

So it was in this frame of mind that I sat in math class seven months after my last encounter with my dad. There was a knock at the door and my teacher sprang to answer it. It sounded like Mum to me, I knew her whisper. But why would she have traveled a hundred kilometers to see me just after I had been home for the long weekend? My teacher beckoned me to the door. I stepped outside into the dark hallway to meet my mother. She spoke, confirming my terror: "It's your dad." I walked toward her as she backed weakly away from the classroom. "He's dead," she said to me. I was gazing at her face for any sign of reality, and it came crashing toward me. Her skin was as white as smoke except for the deep red rivers where tears had been staining her face all morning. I looked away and knew that this was real. I felt the ground plunge away from me, and my heart seemed to suck in all the energy in my body. I would have to teach myself how to move again.

For days afterward, I was unable to follow a train of thought or even turn on the water faucet. I couldn't even find a way to recall the deep anger I once had. It all flew away from me the minute he was murdered. What a sickening culture. That distant place that I spent half my youth trying to embrace had killed my father.

I had been aware of the thread of violence in Jamaican society spun by overly aggressive males. It was what left women and their kids alone. Men killed men of their own race. I could explain it through the need of men to hold their expected place in society, which was never met throughout the years of political upheaval. This kind of frustration is easily internalized. You could smell it mingling with ripe fruits in the shady marketplace heat. It was on the face of every man who walked the streets. It had torn through the philosophy of early ska and created a raga of violent musical themes. I listened to it and danced in the island's roughest clubs, where the glint of steel was almost as noticeable as the scent of rum. It was inconceivable to me that all of that had put an end to my father's life. The Kingston newspapers called it the death of "the Gentle Giant." Although I knew another side of him, he was a man who had expressed a need for serenity in life. He didn't deal well with conflict. As could be expected, the newspaper write-ups concentrated on my father's career. In one lengthy article, one line was allotted to a mention of his three children. When I read it, I was surprised by the pathetic gesture. I read photocopies of these papers at a table surrounded by relatives who for the most part I had never met. A few hours earlier I had arrived in Jamaica in a trance. When I peered into the dark humidity for the people who were supposed to pick me up, my surroundings were devoid of mystery. Jamaica was banal, unexciting. Even my new relatives were not part of the island; they were mostly guests. In my father's home, his absence made me feel aloof, as though I had no reference point.

The days I spent in Jamaica to bury my father granted me closure to one thing and one thing only: my father's living days on earth. Many other things were opened up at that time. My half sister, Shauna, and I met for the first time. At first we were too overwhelmed by it all to talk much, but eventually she spoke a bit about her life and filled me in on my half brother, who hadn't come to the island. The high point of our bonding was probably the night of my dad's funeral. A group of family members who were around the same age went out to the bars. When we arrived home drunk to the point of slurring, Shauna and I wrestled with the car key in the ignition until we practically wet ourselves in a hysterical release from the day. I actually felt a closeness to her that I had never had with anyone else; it was subtle, sorrowful, and full of relief. She reminded me of a part of myself that I didn't consciously know was there. I guess that is because we shared a father. But at times when we had to take care of the business concerning my father's estate, like sifting through his chaotic house for life insurance policies or any other important belongings, I was struck by how different from me my sister was.

My sister is eight years my senior. My brother is five years older. Their lives intersected with my father's at a different time than mine did. He was married to their mother, Joan, and was a part of their family until he and Joan separated when Shauna was a toddler. I certainly do not know the whole story of their relationship, but since my mother was involved with my dad just after he separated from Joan, I have heard some of my mum's perspective. She told me that Joan wanted to continue the marriage and was deeply resentful of my mother. After much turmoil (which included Joan entering my father and mother's apartment one night, threatening to kill), an agreement was reached: my dad would give Joan a second child, and she would promise to leave them alone. This event is such a part of my heart even though it happened outside my lifetime. On the one hand, I am appalled at these three adults for making that choice. On the other hand, I understand my mother's consuming love for my father, a Jamaican woman's claim on the ideal of a Jamaican family, and my father's fragmented devotion to both. Out of this was born a boy, my half brother, who remains a surreal figure in my life. I have yet to meet him.

Returning to Canada after burying my father brought a sense of relief. I sat in the plane draped over the armrest, watching the red earth plunge deep into the panorama. As the misty vegetation and hints of motion tipped away from me, I blocked out the sounds of Kingston that trickled through my swollen mind. I was becoming set on making my life whole. The hours I spent flying gave me a chance to let go of a lot. The sun was an exquisite reassurance among the clouds, but I felt no sorrow when it was time for it to disappear. Things would eventually be fine, even better than I could have imagined. I no longer had an unattainable life to entice me when I wasn't fulfilled. It would be impossible for me to be a part of Jamaican culture, both because I now despised it and because my dad was gone.

I haven't been back to Jamaica since my father's death. Four years later, the grief over my father's death is still a factor in deciding what to do with my future. It sometimes determines what kind of day I have and has given me an increased sensitivity to violence in society. I get angry with my dad, mostly when I feel the financial strain of my life closing in on me and realize that a lot of it could have been relieved if he were alive. Whether it would compensate for the pain he added to my life I can't answer, and I will never know how our relationship would have evolved. I do feel a deep connection to him, sometimes through an almost tangible presence that feels like him, but more often through the work I do and want to continue doing.

Environmental engineering was my dad's field. He did some very important things for the protection of Jamaica's nature, and it makes me sad that he can't continue his work, because it is important. I am comforted by my own interest in environmental protection; I know I will make changes. I am also scared because my passion is often powerful and I don't want to end up submerged in my career with no room for anything else.

It's funny because I'm also following my mother's footsteps through my writing. Encouraging a child to express herself is the best gift a parent can give. My mother is always interested in my creative side, and I in hers. We still fight, but we also share joy and humor that more than make up for it. When I am too hard on myself, she can help me get things in perspective. My mother is a sometimes wildly emotional person, and she has a core that is stronger than iron. She gets things done through thick and thin, and has an amazing capacity for empathy. The pros and cons to this I know well; she gets tired and ill. But I accept the power she has bestowed on me as a great tool for my future.

I am open to the future, and I feel more directed than I have in a long time. I know the way that life can surprise us. I have a lot ahead of me.

Unfortunately, the family I come from is split right now. There are relatives on both sides with whom I have rocky relationships at best. On my father's side, some have shown no interest in finding out who I am, and others send me cards once in awhile. I haven't heard anything from my sister in months. I don't even know for sure where she and my brother are.

By looking at my life as a product of two ethnicities, I have learned about what ethnicity means to many people, and I have learned what it means to me. I know racism; I know how many mixed people choose to be black because it's easier. I know white people who prefer it that way too. I am reluctant to resign myself to one side or the other, which shows up in many aspects of myself. I am neither black nor white, but I can be both. The strongest ethnic ties I feel are to others with the same heritage.

After Dartmouth, Lola went on to universities in two major Canadian cities, where she fostered a culturally diverse second adult "family" of friends. Her career has often focused on international topics, and her work has brought her to encounters with various cultures, including residencies on three different continents. She lives with her partner and they share a son, who is of a similar mix of Jamaican and Canadian heritage.

About the Editors

Andrew Garrod is a professor emeritus at Dartmouth College, where he previously chaired the Department of Education, directed the Teacher Education Program, and taught courses in adolescence, moral development, and contemporary issues in U.S. education. He currently directs a teaching volunteer program in the Marshall Islands in the central Pacific and has conducted a research project in Bosnia and Herzegovina over a number of years. His recent publications include the coedited books *Mi Voz, Mi Vida: Latino College Students Tell Their Life Stories*, *Balancing Two Worlds: Asian American College Students Tell Their Life Stories*, and the seventh edition of *Adolescent Portraits: Identity, Relationships, and Challenges*. With Robert Kilkenny, he has coedited an anthology on growing up Muslim. In 1991 and 2009 he was awarded Dartmouth College's Distinguished Teaching Award.

Robert Kilkenny is a clinical associate in the School of Social Work at Simmons College in Boston. He is coeditor of *Souls Looking Back: Life Stories of Growing Up Black*, *Balancing Two Worlds: Asian American College Students Tell Their Life Stories*, *Mi Voz, Mi Vida: Latino College Students Tell Their Life Stories*, and *Adolescent Portraits: Identity, Relationships, and Challenges*, which is in its seventh edition. With Andrew Garrod, he has coedited an anthology about growing up Muslim. He is the founder and executive director of the Alliance for Inclusion and Prevention, a public-private partnership providing school-based mental health, special education, and after-school programs to at-risk students in the Boston public schools.

Christina Gómez is a professor of sociology and Latino and Latin American studies at Northeastern Illinois University in Chicago. She holds an MBA from the University of Chicago Booth School of Business and a Ph.D. in sociology from Harvard University. She has received numerous prizes and fellowships, including the Henry Luce Scholars Fellowship. Her research has concentrated on racial identity construction in the United States, discrimination, and immigration. She is the author of articles that focus on such topics as skin color discrimination among Latinos, the construction of Latino identity, and the politics of bilingual education. She is also one of the editors of *Mi Voz, Mi Vida: Latino College Students Tell Their Life Stories* (2007), a book of essays written by students about growing up Latino in this country. Her current research examines undocumented immigrant university students.